The Lost Art

Boundary Books Cricket History Series - No.1

The Lost Art
A History of Under-arm Bowling

by

GERALD BRODRIBB

Boundary Books

For my grandson, James, who once banned my underarm twiddlers

Other Cricket Books by Gerald Brodribb

The English Game

Cricket in Fiction

Champions of Cricket

Some Memorable Bowling

Some Memorable Innings

All Round the Wicket

The Book of Cricket Verse

A Yankee Looks at Cricket

Hit For Six

The Art of Nicholas Felix

Cricket at Hastings

Next Man In

Felix on the Bat

The Croucher

Maurice Tate

Boundary Books Ltd
Southlands, Goostrey, Cheshire, CW4 8NT

First published 1997

© Gerald Brodribb, 1997

ISBN 0 9522070 8 7

Contents

Acknowledgements

I am most grateful to all those who in different ways have helped me in this story of a somewhat esoteric subject, which is surely part of the history of the game. Particular thanks go to Michael Brearley who has kindly provided a Foreword. Thanks also to the following; the late Tom Barling, Scyld Berry, the late G.B.Cuthbertson, Alex Davies, John Dew, R.N.Exton, Philip Hawkins, Tony Lewis, Tony Millgan, Don Oslear, the late Grahame Parker, Irving Rosenwater, Peter Wynne-Thomas, and Tony Wesson. Roger Mann has provided a number of photographs.

Gerald Brodribb

Ewhurst Green, January 1997

Foreword

MIKE BREARLEY, O.B.E.

One of cricket's charms is its range of skills and the range of physiques and styles which deliver the skills. I am glad that people of such varied shapes and sizes as Vishwanath and Ambrose, Adams and Milburn have all graced international cricket.

We should resist tendencies for the game to become stereotyped. As a 21 year old I bowled under-arm in first-class cricket. It was not done as a joke or a protest or to belittle anyone. I thought it might disconcert the batsman when ordinary methods had failed. The skills of under-arm bowling, which must have been considerable, were by then utterly unfamiliar.

However, though I did practise (a bit), my skills were extremely moderate, and the person I most disconcerted was our Cambridge wicket-keeper, Mike Griffith. He was, I think, embarrassed by me; so much so that he missed a stumping.

I too was a bit intimidated by the conservative and critical attitudes of others in and around the game. That is one reason why I did not develop the skills of under-arm or lob bowling. It seemed not worth riding the opposition which was often intense.

But who knows? The day of the lob bowler might yet come again. I am inclined to agree with Gerald Brodribb that these nice, antiquated oddities should be preserved.

Chapter 1

Early Days

In the early days of cricket the batsman defended a wide shallow wicket consisting of two stumps and one long bail, in all measuring 2ft wide by 1ft high. Since the bowler trundled or 'bowled' the ball along the ground towards the wicket, the bat was curved rather like a hockey stick and the variety of strokes was most limited. As time went on, the bowler began to realise that if he made the ball bounce it was more difficult to defend the wicket, so in reply the batsman began to employ a straighter bat with which he could more easily counter the rising ball. Consequently the wicket changed shape by becoming tall and narrow instead of shallow and wide. All this evolution took a long time.

After incidents in which the ball had gone straight between the two uprights without dislodging the bail (which was counted as 'not out'), a third centre stump was added in 1776. Though the addition of this stump was obviously fairer to the bowler, there was some protesting that it might tend to shorten the game and also make the batsmen too cautious.

The whole story of cricket is that of an unending contest between bat and ball. Once the bowler had developed a ball that pitched and lifted instead of rolling along the ground the batsman had to learn new methods. John Small's creation of a straight bat in 1775 helped the batsman to master forward play to counter the length of the delivery. We are extremely lucky to have evidence of the early development of cricket in the writings of John Nyren who recorded the doings of the Hambledon Club in the latter end of the eighteenth century. Hambledon was not the earliest of known cricket clubs since there is evidence of the Vine Club at Sevenoaks and of other clubs being active as early as the 1740s, but it was the first club to have its cricket and cricketers recorded by an able writer, and this has provided a wide-ranging picture of cricket as played at that time.

Among the Hambledon cricketers was David Harris (1753-1803) whom John Nyren claimed to be 'the best bowler ever known'. The following long description of him is taken from Nyren's book, *Cricketers of My Time*, as edited by Charles Cowden Clarke. It was published in 1833, some forty years after the activities of the Hambledon cricketers it describes. Here is Nyren's study of the bowler:

"Harris was a muscular, bony man, standing about 5' 9 1/2" in height. It would be difficult, perhaps impossible, to convey in writing an accurate idea of the grand effect of Harris's bowling; they only, who have played against him, can fully appreciate it. His attitude when preparing his run previously to delivering the ball would have made a beautiful study for a sculptor. Pheidias would certainly have taken him for a model. First of all he stood erect like a soldier at drill; then with a graceful curve of the arm, he raised the ball to his forehead, and drawing back his right foot, started off with his left. The calm look and the general air of the man were uncommonly striking, and from this series of preparation he never deviated.

"His mode of delivering the ball was very singular. He would bring it from under the arm by a twist and nearly as high as his armpit, and with this action push it, as it were, from him. How it was that the balls acquired the velocity they did by this mode of delivery, I never could comprehend. . . . In the prime of his playing he very rarely gave a toss, although the balls were pitched a full length. In bowling he never stooped in the least in his delivery, but kept himself upright all the time. His balls were very little beholden to the ground when pitched; it was but a touch and up again, and woe be to the man who did not get in to block them, for they had such a peculiar curve that they would ground his fingers against the bat. . . . He was considerably faster than Lambert, and so superior in style and finish that I can draw no comparison between them."

There is a set of sketches of the Hambledon players made by George Shepherd in about 1790; one of these shows Harris in his upright bowling position, but even from this and from Nyren's description it is not easy to visualise the delivery or to realise its elegance. It seems that the ball must have been delivered with some thrusting or jerking motion which raises doubts about its legality under present law. If Harris was the best of the Hambledon bowlers, others must surely have followed his methods, and the batsmen for all their straight bats must have had plenty of problems, as the slower bowlers were now able to produce some spin or 'bias' from leg, and the bowling of Lamborn provided the first recorded evidence of off-spin.

Another man of Hambledon was showing even greater enterprise. Tom Walker (1762-1831) was known as 'Old Everlasting' with his "hard ungainly scrag of mutton frame and wilted apple-John face with long spider legs". He showed sound skills of defence - the prototype opening batsman - and he was one of the few who could cope with Harris' bowling, even though "his knuckles were handsomely knocked about" by him. Walker's experiments with bowling were even more important than his great batting powers. In about 1788 he experimented with a ball jerked at such a "frightful pace" that it was banned; later he realised that a ball delivered with the arm raised sideways could cause considerable problems for the batsman, but the Hambledon Club also instantly outlawed this pioneer of round-arm bowling as 'foul play'. Walker was not one to argue or to be dismayed; he still had ideas, and now instead of sending the ball down at the usual pace he tried bowling slower balls lobbed up in the air; they acquired some 'flight', sometimes with a touch of 'bias' which severely puzzled the batsman. Poor Walker had critics even for this slow harmless-looking bowling. After his lobs had helped England to defeat Kent by 10 runs in 1792, William Beldham, "Silver Billy", the greatest batsman of his time, was almost apologetic, and stated with some regret for Walker's success, "I feel so ashamed of such baby bowling."

But Walker was no doubt the forerunner of the genuine slow lob bowler. There have been many types of underarm bowling. There is the daisy-cutting fast grub which can achieve considerable pace, the Harris-type of ball with its nip off the pitch, the slow flighted ball with spin applied, the carefully placed 'bodyline' full toss to invite a leg-side catch, and at times the monstrously tossed up donkey-drop intended to land on top of the stumps. The truly skilled lob bowler will become master of all these deliveries.

By the turn of the century Hambledon cricket was fading, but there was increasing interest in the game in the London area, and this produced some notable players. Mr E. H. Budd (1785-1875) and William Lambert (1779-1851) not only batted with outstanding success (Lambert in 1817 was the first man ever to score two hundreds in a match), but they also became the two leading bowlers of the day. According to James Pycroft, the cricket historian, Budd, against whom he had often played, delivered the ball from the hip, with a little chuck or fling from the hand, and Lambert and Warsop of Nottingham also bowled in the same manner. Since Tom Walker's abortive experiment of extending the arm sideways, others must have been ready to try this very effective method, but all such attempts at round-arm bowling were heavily frowned upon.

3

Another contemporary champion was the autocratic Lord Frederick Beauclerk who as well as following Beldham as the best batsman, bowled his underarms with a cunning matched later by William Clarke. To quote the old Hambledon batsman, Thomas Beagley, "He did find out a man's hit very soon, and set his field to foil it. He could make the ball get up and look at you."

If the legend is to be believed, John Willes, of Sutton Valence, came to adopt round-arm bowling in a most unusual way. He often used to practice batting to the bowling of his sister Christina. She wore a wide hooped dress, which meant that she could deliver the ball only by raising her arm sideways. John Willes found such a delivery awkward to play, and so decided to bowl in this way himself. His first recorded match was the first-ever Gentlemen v Players match, at Lord's in 1806. Tom Walker was also playing but it is doubtful if they discussed round-arm bowling. Soon after, Willes produced his new delivery in public. It was effective, but met with such opposition that some teams refused to play against him. To quote H. S. Altham, "He played sometimes with much uproar and confusion. . . still he would persevere until the ring closed on the players, the stumps were lawlessly pulled up, and all came to a standstill."

But Willes continued his roundarms with missionary zeal until it all ended on July 15 1822. When he opened the bowling for Kent v MCC he was promptly no-balled, possibly under official instructions. To quote H. S. Altham again, "He threw down the ball in disgust, jumped on his horse, and rode away out of Lord's and out of cricket history." Others, however, continued to champion his cause, so perhaps Christina Willes played a real part in sounding the death knell of the 'old-fashioned' underarm bowling.

MCC had become the official administrators of the Laws of cricket, and just before 1811 it was laid down that the ball must be bowled under-hand and be delivered with the hand below the elbow. This was the first real attempt to put a stop to round-arm experiments which were condemned as 'throwing' bowling by those who hated what seemed to be a revolutionary practice. (Though the early Laws and mid-Victorian writers such as Pycroft refer to under-hand bowling, it seems more logical to use the term under-arm bowling, as opposed to round-arm and over-arm.) In this book the term 'lob' is synonymous with under-arm.

Nicholas Felix was an ardent opposer of any new type of bowling and wrote, "Underhand bowling is the oldest of all, and indeed the only legitimate style; all

4

innovations and deviations from it are more or less objectionable." William Ward, the greatest batsman of the day, who scored 278 against Norfolk at Lord's in 1820, was another adamant conservative and he urged MCC to stress the condition of 'hand below the elbow' in a Law that in full reads in such a complex way that Col. R. S. Rait-Kerr in his admirable book *The Laws of Cricket* (1950) quotes it as an example of how not to frame a Law. The poor umpires who then lacked the present status of authority and could not risk offending their masters must have been sorely perplexed, and attempts at 'illegal' round-arm bowling continued to flourish more according to the attitude of the captains than that of the umpires.

By 1827 opinion was much divided, and there were many who felt that the great improvement in batting needed to be countered by the bowler being allowed more freedom of delivery. As a result special trial games were arranged in which the bowlers William Lillywhite and James Broadbridge, both of Sussex, were allowed to demonstrate the ways of round-arm bowling. The only result of these trials was that though the Law was simplified it still insisted that hand and arm were kept 'below the elbow'. The round-armers tended to take no notice of this, and confusion continued amongst everyone including the umpires, who frequently turned a blind eye on what seemed an obvious breach of the Law. To no-ball a fellow player was a drastic action, and many umpires were themselves probably in favour of more scope for bowlers. The traditionalists were losing the battle, and when a major revision of the Laws was made in 1835 a further concession was made to bowlers in that they could now raise the arm as high as shoulder level.

Around this time the Rev. John Mitford, editor of *The Gentlemens' Magazine* and a cricket fanatic, came across the veteran William Fennex and befriended him. Fennex had been a cricketer in the early 1800s and had been an expert in single-wicket challenges. Mitford got him talking, and in reference to the new style round-arm bowling, the old man, who used to bowl fast under-arm with a very high action, stated, "You see, sir, my bowling would be queer if I were a younger man, but some of our older bowlers, much as it is the fashion to despise the fair under-hand bowling, would rip up your present players in no time at all. Indeed, people have no notion of what the best of the old under-hand bowlers could do." This was a firm reminder of the value of true under-hand bowling at a time when many bowlers were rushing wildly to take advantage of the new round-arm legislation; it had opened the floodgates to a mass of bowlers who were hurling the ball down usually from round the wicket, and their lack of control produced countless wides.

5

The best and fairest of the new round-arm bowlers was Alfred Mynn (1807-1861) who worked up a great pace off a short run and is said to have made the ball hum as it went down. It must have seemed at the time that this round-arm revolution would mean the ending of all under-arm bowling; (did not the recent obsession with hostile speed bowling once threaten the extinction of spinners?). Certainly the general decline in under-arm bowling must date from the mid 1830s, but this old-fashioned delivery was far from finished. For one type of under-arm bowling, however, this was virtually the end in big cricket, namely the 'grub' ball, delivered fast along the ground in a manner common enough in the early days.

Some of the old underarm bowlers could achieve considerable pace, and one of the fastest of all was George Brown of Sussex (1783-1837), who was considered slightly faster than the earlier - highly colourful - George Osbaldeston. In a volume of *Scores and Biographies* (Vol. 1, 1862, p415) there was a most interesting survey in which it was stated that for sheer speed Brown and Osbaldeston could be bracketed with three later round-arm bowlers, W. Marcon and H.W. and W. Fellows. In pace these five stood ahead of the next group of T. Brett (under-arm), A. Mynn, J. Jackson and T. Sherman. It is surprising to see that the editor, Arthur Haygarth, reckoned that several under-arm bowlers could rival round-armers for pace. Fast under-arm balls bowled with all-out venom could be very effective, especially under certain conditions. As W. Bolland wrote in 1852, "Skimming bowling often tells well on a hard, uneven or glibby ground", but he went on to say that to watch such fast bowling all the time would be tedious, as well we know.

To return to George Brown, a contemporary report describes his effects in a single-wicket match in which 'Squire' Osbaldeston was also playing:

"After Brown had bowled for a little while, Osbaldeston said, 'You won't keep that pace long, I know.' 'Oh, yes,' said Brown, 'I can bowl like that all day if you like', and he did bowl in that fashion for four hours and a half without intermission. Off 230 of his balls 8 runs were made. When he went in, he drove the first ball through a paling and across a lane that ran outside the ground. Brown was an uncommonly powerful man, and a regular 'hitter' though not a fine bat. His arm was said to be as large round as an ordinary man's leg, and proportionately muscular. So tremendous was his pace, that he always had two long-stops, and generally all the field behind the wickets . . . at Lord's a man once tried to stop the ball with his coat, but Brown   bowled right through it, killing a dog instantly."

The killing of the poor dog is perhaps mythical, but his speed was deadly, and the wicket-keeper was wise enough to protect himself with a vest made up of a sack packed with straw. The two long-stops must have been kept very busy with the many snicks, tips and byes resulting from Brown's bowling. When a ball from Brown hit the wicket strange things happened. The Bishop of St Andrews (the son of Wordsworth the poet) affirmed that at Brighton he once saw a ball hit the stumps in such a way that both bails somehow flew <u>back</u> as far as the bowler's wicket. Since with Brown's bowling most of the fielders were placed behind the line of the stumps, it was tempting to the batsman to try and push the ball into the open spaces, but you had to stand up to the bowling, and that without the protection of pads or gloves. The indomitable William Ward at Lord's once stood firm and poked the ball away for singles; since Brown was reluctant to do any chasing, one or two fielders were brought forward of the wicket.

Brown was once mastered by the Hambledon hero William Beldham when England were playing Hampshire at Lord's in 1819. Against the Hampshire attack, which included Brown's fiercesome pace, aided perhaps by what Pycroft called 'an undetected jerk', Beldham was quite undaunted, and despite his age of 53, scored 72 out of the England total of 177. He hit Brown so freely that, to quote *Scores and Biographies*, "at last Brown was afraid to bowl to him." According to John Mitford, "it mattered not who bowled to him or how he bowled, fast or slow, high or low, straight or bias; away flew the ball from the bat, like an eagle on the wing." Beldham was a man of courage as well as skill, and this was one of his finest innings. Before the match someone warned him about the danger of Brown's bowling, to which he replied dryly that he supposed that he would still be allowed to have a bat to assist him.

A possible replica of the manner of Brown's deliveries may lie in the bowling of a certain butcher named W. Crowhurst as recalled by C. B. Fry from his boyhood days at Chislehurst in the late 1870s. Crowhurst bowled so fast that, like Brown, he needed two long-stops. He played for the West Kent Club and some local teams refused to play against him. C. B. Fry told G. D. Martineau that Crowhurst used "a low-level, straight-down under-hand swing, with a straight arm, putting a heavy momentum into the delivery and a decided follow-through." He played in one county match for Kent against Nottinghamshire at Canterbury in 1877 and opened the bowling but took only one wicket. When one of his fast sneak balls hit Richard Daft on the foot, the batsman turned to Lord Harris, the Kent captain, and said: "This is not cricket, my Lord, this is not cricket."

Another excellent description of the manner of such bowling concerns a successful bowler in Canada in 1872. His name was Bullock and the report reads, "His style is very swift, very straight under-arm grounders, the ball usually taking the ground about 3 to 6 feet from his hand, and hopping an indefinite number of times before it arrives at the popping crease, although an occasional full one for the batsman's person or over his head may be looked for."

It would be most interesting if some of the present day giant fast bowlers were to try the experiment of delivering the ball in the manner of those fast under-armers of old.

Though a few grubbers remained, including Alfred Walker, the second of the famous family, who bowled 'fast daisy-cutters' for Cambridge University in 1846-8, in time the fast delivery that went all along the ground came to be regarded as undesirable and even unfair. The terms daisy-cutter, grub and sneak showed the poor reputation of such a ball and it died out of big cricket, though occasionally we hear of a brief revival. C. I. Thornton in the 1870s sometimes indulged in such bowling and once took 4-36 for Cambridge University v Surrey who were not pleased. An editorial in the magazine *Cricket* made this comment, "C. I. Thornton reintroduced genuine daisy-cutters into first-class cricket. I remember Cambridge meeting Surrey in 1870. Jupp and Dick Humphrey had notched a century in the second hands and seemed likely to stop. C.I. was called up and sent down some twenty bouncers, which didn't pitch anything like halfway. With them he took three wickets before a run was scored off him. Everyone was amused, and the Surrey batsmen not a trifle disgusted by being dismissed at 'such balls'. Was it not H. H. Stephenson who tried to retaliate when Cambridge went in? But somehow he hadn't the knack."

This confrontation with C. I. Thornton provoked Stephenson to tell him that he ought to be ashamed to call himself a bowler - "Why, you wouldn't bowl me out in two years!" Thornton took up the challenge and always had a go at Stephenson whenever the chance arose, but Stephenson managed to keep his wicket intact. Then, only a few days after the two-year time limit was up, they met again in a match at Richmond, and such was the irony of fate that Thornton clean bowled Stephenson - just too late to win the challenge.

Here is a further note on the matter by Frederick Gale: "During last season (1870) Mr Thornton went on with quick daisy-cutters and down fell the players' wickets, some of them complaining that it was not fair cricket. When so many instances of this kind crop up from time to time, the fair inference is that cricket gets into a groove, and the same kind of cricket is played everywhere for a time until a sudden novelty puts everyone out. True it is that masters of the art very soon find out the difficulty and overcome it, but if we are so much better now than we ever were, nothing ought to take us by surprise."

George Brann, that fine Sussex batsman, in his later days sometimes bowled fast grubs for fun but the disappearance of the daisy cutter in first-class cricket was inevitable. Even so, writing in 1890, A. G. Steel said that such a delivery might still be in use in village cricket and lesser games, but he added the proviso that whenever used it would be likely to create ill-feeling.

So long as it was the only kind of bowling there was no real need to have any special name for under-arm bowling. The reference to lob seems to be first found in the pages of Mary Russell Mitford's *Our Village* of 1824, when she wrote, "The change from Long's lobbing to Simmons' fast balls posed them completely", but the term lob seems not to have been freely used until it occurs in Pycroft's book *The Cricket Field* of 1851. Even in later years under-arm balls are sometimes referred to as 'slows' which sometimes makes the identification of the type of bowling difficult. Terminology can be confusing. Even recently we have seen the word 'lobs' wrongly used to mean slow tossed-up over-arm balls.

The legislation of 1835 had enabled the true round-arm 'under the shoulder' bowler to flourish, but many realised that they could be even more effective if they illegally raised the arm even higher above the shoulder level. This created more problems for the umpires that lasted for another 30 years, until in 1864 all restrictions were lifted. It seems a long time for such an important matter to be resolved and it led to a great deal of controversy. In cricket reports for the 1850s, for example, we read that so-and-so bowler's action "would surely not be permitted if he played at Lord's", and sometimes there is a warning that a certain bowler may not be asked to play for the team in future unless he mended his ways. This threat apparently caused some bowlers to lower the arm to a legal level, but it rather depended where he was playing and who was the umpire. It was all most unsatisfactory and it is a wonder that the game withstood such continuous strife.

While the realists were confident that a batsman would surely be able to adapt even to full over-arm bowling, the old traditionalists continued to condemn what they mistakenly called 'throwing' bowling, which in fact it was not. Whereas the new round-armers tended to use a genuine straight-arm delivery (the main feature of a fair ball), many of the old-style under-hand bowlers, including Harris and later William Clarke, seemed to have delivered the ball with a 'push' or jerk that might well offend the Law. In other words it was the old under-arm bowlers who seem to have done the 'throwing' and not the new style round-armers, who were being accused of this.

Some of the new breed of fast round-arm bowlers found it difficult to keep on the target, and even some of the under-arm bowlers were wildly inaccurate. Tom Barker, the old Notts player and later a famous umpire, used to tell of an under-arm fast bowler, who on one occasion could not get a length. He kept sending ball after ball right over the batsman's head, so Barker advised him to go back an extra yard or two, but this did not seem to make much difference. 'Go further back yet', said Barker. He did so and at last managed to bowl full pitches, so he went even further back for his delivery behind the crease, and eventually went so far that he managed to bowl down the wicket at his own end.

But though the new round-arm fashion spread rapidly, some clubs continued with the under-arm delivery, and when the Manchester Club played MCC in a match at Lord's in 1842, they employed only under-arm bowlers. To quote *Bell's Life*, "the MCC gentlemen had much amusement in hitting them away."

Chapter 2

William Clarke

William Clarke (1798-1856) had one of the strangest careers ever known. Born at Nottingham on Christmas Eve, the son of a cricket-loving brick-layer, he gradually established himself as a slow under-arm bowler, though the flood of round-arm bowlers after the legislation in 1827 must have limited his chances, and for a long time little was known of him outside his own county. He had learnt his art from another Nottinghamshire bowler of the old school, Sam Warsop, and he also acknowledged much benefit from the example of William Lambert.

It was not until 1836, when he was aged 38, that Clarke first appeared at Lord's, representing the North against the South. His next game at Lord's was not until 1843, when he was aged nearly 45. He was soon showing that his skill could obtain wickets at all levels of the game; for Nottinghamshire against Kent in 1845 at Trent Bridge he had analyses of 9 - 29 and 7 - 40, and of these 16 wickets 9 were clean bowled and 2 hit-wicket. Later, at Canterbury when bowling for England *v* Kent, he took another 12 wickets, 3 of them in 3 balls, though such a feat was not then called a hat-trick. At long last people in the south realised that this elderly, one-eyed, old-fashioned lob bowler was a force to be reckoned with.

The result was that Clarke was invited to join the MCC bowling staff - a high honour - and also in 1846 he made his first appearance for the Players at Lord's, and celebrated it with figures of 5 - 30 in the Gentlemen's first innings. To play in this prestigious game - the most important one of the season - was almost the equivalent of today winning a representative cap. He was to be picked for this game for every season until 1854, and in those 8 games he took 38 wickets. In 1847 he and William Lillywhite - the round-arm pioneer, now aged 55 - shared the bowling honours against the Gentlemen, bowling unchanged, with Clarke taking 11 -36. But in Clarke's own opinion the happiest day of his life was July 17, 1845, when he had the great Fuller Pilch stumped for 7, and then clean bowled first Alfred Mynn and then Felix - both for 0. The three best batsmen in England were thus all dismissed in a matter of a few minutes.

When he first appeared at Lord's, Clarke was facing batsmen who in recent years had had little experience of under-arm bowling, which had been pushed out of fashion by the round-arm explosion. They completely underestimated Clarke's extreme skill, and the general feeling was "We'll knock this rubbish out of the field." When he was first told about Clarke's revival of lob bowling, Fuller Pilch, the Number One batsman of the day, was said to have commented, "Gentlemen, I think you might put me in on Monday morning, and get me out by about Saturday night", but having eventually faced Clarke, Pilch changed his tune completely, and though he played Clarke better than anyone else, with his fine forward play, he admitted that he never really mastered him.

When Clarke joined the Lord's staff in 1846 he was already known as 'Old' Clarke, and he was no doubt at first subjected to much mockery by those who considered his bowling would be easy meat. At such an advanced age he might well have been thinking of retirement, but it was in that same year that he first put into action his enterprising idea of collecting together a team of the top players in England and touring with them all over the country, spreading the gospel of cricket and at the same time lining his own pocket. The tours of his England Eleven were a real success, though it meant that these star players were continually playing teams of odds, even up to sides of XXII players. This was the only way to make a game of it, and very often the local sides had also to be fortified by 'given men', usually high-class professional bowlers who often severely troubled the England batsmen.

Clarke, as captain, gave himself every opportunity of bowling, and he had an enormous appetite for wickets. The historians have calculated that in the seven seasons 1848-1854 Clarke took 2327 wickets, the biggest haul being 476 wickets in 1854. Though the majority of these wickets were taken against odds, when Clarke played in first-class matches he produced similar performances. Contemporary opinion held that he stood in a class by himself.

Consider the reasons for such success; his under-arm bowling came as a puzzling novelty to batsmen now constantly used to facing round-armers and they did not know how to cope with it. Even a very moderate lob bowler instantly sets up mental problems for the batsman who feels that he is honour-bound to smash 'such rubbish', and yet is terrified of the humiliation of getting out to it. Clarke also had a certain advantage not available to his successors in bowling under-arm, since in his day any deliberate attempt to hit straight balls to leg was considered improper until E. M. Grace and others showed that such convention was sheer nonsense. Also, it was not then thought to be the right thing to advance down the wicket to attack. The famous umpire Bob Thoms made the following observations about this:

"Clarke had an immense advantage over Mr Walker (a later under-arm bowler) for when he was enjoying his summer-time he had to bowl to fast-footed batsmen. It was considered *infra dig.* to go out to him, though many men knew well enough that it would be the best way to play him. I remember that Joe Guy said to me, "I could do the jump right enough, but they don't like you to do it," whereas when Mr Walker was at his best all this had been altered. Just think what a vast difference this means to a bowler! What took the stuffing out of Old Clarke was the way in which Julius Caesar and one or two others stepped out to him, and knocked him all over the place."

When Nicholas Felix first met Clarke he ran out and attacked him in a brilliant innings of 54, and when they next met Felix's entry was hailed with the cry, "Here comes Clarke's master!": But Clarke had remembered Felix's tactics, put the ball over his head as he advanced and bowled him. Felix was never again to master Clarke, for he had stored in his memory Felix's approach, and practised all the winter a ball which he knew would defeat him. That epitomises Clarke's skill and powers of observation, and his realisation that a batsman who threatened to attack him must instantly be checked.

Another reason for Clarke's success was that whereas the round-armer could get little break on the ball, Clarke could get plenty of turn, or what was then called 'bias', so much so that when bowling at Lord's he preferred to bowl from the Pavilion end since otherwise the helpful slope produced too much turn. Pycroft said that some malformation in Clarke's arm assisted this bias. But the chief reason for Clarke taking so many wickets was his almost uncanny astuteness in summing up a batsman's weakness and playing upon it. Never can there have been a more cunning bowler, and Haygarth rightly called him 'fox-headed'; I suppose that W.G. Grace and, in later years, C.V. Grimmett - both slow, round-arm bowlers - showed some of the same skill in luring a batsman to destruction.

It is not easy to know just how Clarke delivered the ball, and there seem to be conflicting accounts; no doubt he used to vary his methods according to circumstances. Here are a few observations, beginning with that from Richard Daft:

"Clarke's delivery was a peculiar one. He came up to the crease with that usual 'trot' which nearly all slow under-hand bowlers adopt, but instead of delivering the ball at the height of, or between, his hip, he at the last moment bent back his elbow, bringing the ball almost under his right armpit, and delivered the ball thus from as great a height as it was possible to attain, and still be under-hand. He was by this delivery able to make the ball get up higher and quicker from the pitch than he would have done if he had delivered it in the same way as other lob bowlers. I have heard old cricketers say that they have received from Clarke many balls that got up quite 'nasty' from the pitch, with a lot of screw on them. He seldom bowled two balls alike and could vary his pace and pitch in a wonderful manner. He was able to detect the weak points of a batsman quicker, perhaps, than any bowler that ever lived."

This delivery seems to resemble that of David Harris; another comment was that it was reminiscent of someone throwing a quoit.

Another contemporary, William Caffyn, believed that batsmen were puzzled not so much by Clarke's natural break as by the problems of his fast ball; "You couldn't see it coming until it was almost up to you, and it was the fear of this ball which made you hesitate to go out and hit the slow ones. I really think that this was the bottom of his success."

Clarke himself wrote: "My success depends not on what is called good length, but on the exact pitch, the one 'blind spot' according to the reach and style of the player. . . also I can vary the pace without betraying the change by my action." This means that Clarke had not only extreme powers of observation, but also total control over the ball which enabled him to put it exactly where he wanted to. Such accuracy was maintained by constant winter practice.

This full survey of Clarke's performance is well justified for the most successful underarm bowler in cricket history. One of his maxims tells it all; he once wrote, "Bowling consists of two parts; there is the mechanical part and the intellectual part. First, you want the hand to pitch where you please; and then the head to know where to pitch, according to the player."

14

Clarke died in 1856, and it was quite in character that he should take a wicket with the last ball he ever delivered. In that same year a young cricketer made his debut at Lord's. He was V.E. Walker, one of six cricketing brothers, and from then on he was seen in big cricket until his last game in 1877. Here is his own account of how he became a lob bowler; it comes from an interview with 'Old Ebor' in the late 1890s:

"Lob bowling was to me an acquired art, adopted through the exigencies of school cricket. I once used to bowl round-arm, with a medium pace. The Hon. Robert Grimston and Lord Bessborough who used to coach us at Harrow, got me to take up lob bowling for the good of the school team. I used to bowl rather fast lobs, too, with a high delivery. I had a habit of running well up the pitch after the ball, and that got me a number of wickets. Of course batsmen think it beneath their dignity to be bowled by a lob, which reminds me of an amusing incident in which 'Ducky' Diver was concerned. It was in a North v South match, and somehow I managed to knock off his bails. He was so wild that he turned round and knocked his three stumps out of the ground before retiring to the pavilion. He was sorry for this afterwards and apologised for losing his temper. . . . My 10 wickets in an innings were for the Gentlemen of Middlesex v the Gentlemen of Kent on June 16, 1864, and for Middlesex against Lancashire at Manchester in July 1865. Against the Kent Gentlemen, the 10 wickets cost 37 runs: the 10 Lancastrians cost 104 runs. I must admit, however, that the batsmen got their own back sometimes: I had to put up with as much 'snuff' as any bowler in my time."

Walker had previously discussed with 'Old Ebor' the third of his all-ten-wickets feats. It was when playing for England v Surrey at the Oval in 1859. England batted first and were all out for 172, Walker aged only 22, scoring 20*. Surrey were then out for 131, Walker taking all ten wickets for 74 runs. He writes: "The curious part of the bowling feat was that when the last man came in, Julius Caesar, who was ninth on the list, was missed off my bowling. I thought at the time that I was just going to miss the ten wickets feat, but I got the other fellow, Granny Martingell, caught by Wisden, and thus accomplished the performance I wanted to do. My success struck me as singular at the time, because the bowler at the other end was far greater than I, namely John Jackson."

In one over Walker captured the wickets of Burbidge, Caffyn and Stephenson off the 1st, 3rd and 4th balls. In their second innings England batted well all through for a score of 390, of which the top score was a chanceless 108 by Walker - regarded by him as his best innnings ever. Surrey collapsed utterly in their second innings for only 39 runs: this time Jackson took 6-21, while, bowling unchanged with him, Walker took the other four wickets for 21. He again fielded brilliantly. Walker's all-round performance in this match must be, to quote *Scores and Biographies*, "one of the most wonderful cricketing feats ever achieved."

There was another occasion when Walker nearly achieved a fourth 'ten wickets' feat. When Middlesex met Sussex at Islington in 1864, a the close of the second innings, it at first seemed that Walker had taken all ten wickets for 62 runs. He was highly congratulated, only for it to be discovered that since one of the Sussex batsmen - well out of his ground - had just touched the ball before it rebounded from the wicket-keeper's pads on to the wicket, the decision was altered to 'run out' instead of 'stumped'. Present Law would have considered this a stumping, giving the wicket to Walker.

One contemporary, Edward Rutter, wrote this of Walker's methods: "He was the most formidable customer as a bowler, and the most athletic fellow that I ever saw in the cricket field. I have seen him catch a man behind the batsman's wicket near short-leg which shows, as much as anything I can think of, what a lot of ground he covered. It did not matter to him how hard the ball was driven back to him; if it was within reach he made a catch of it with either hand. His action was peculiar; it was a sort of half-cock action, for his hand, which was higher than the hip when the ball was leaving it, was at some distance from the body - not in the least like Old Clarke, who bowled with his hand high up, but close to his side. Walker always bowled round the wicket, so that the ball came at a considerable angle. But in my opinion the greatest reason for his success in bowling was the way in which he fielded it; he was all over the place. How he managed to get his spin I don't know, but he had enough of it."

Apart from this controlled spin, Walker occasionally indulged in 'an absurdly high ball with parabolic flight'. Another reason for his bowling round the wicket was that it helped him to avoid scraping his knuckles on the stumps, a problem that could always arise with any delivery with the hand held low to the ground. Canon McCormick has added the following comment: "V.E.'s difficulty lay chiefly in his deceptive variation of pace. He was a splendid judge of a batsman's ability and very quickly found out his weak spots. He did not concern himself with averages. His one leading idea was to get a man out."

16

*Above: Francis Hayman's
engraving of cricket in 1748 clearly
shows the original bowling style in
the days before round-arm*

*Left: David Harris, the most
famous bowler from the
Hambledon era*

William Clarke, founder of the All England XI and prince of under-arm bowlers in an age dominated by round-arm

W. W. READ.
BOWING ONE OF
HIS LOBS.

The Oxford Lob-bowler.

Above left: W.W.Read of Surrey and England

Above right: J.B.Wood, the Oxford University lob bowler

Left: Len Braund of Surrey, Somerset and England is not recorded as bowling under-arm in a first-class match but here he demonstrates the technique

THE LEC SPIN.

THE OFF SPIN.

J.H.Piton, the South African lobster, demonstrates the off-spin and leg-spin deliveries

Walker's career began at a time when Clarke's ended, and there were later the inevitable pointless attempts to compare the two. The general feeling of contemporary players was that Clarke was the greater because there was an indescribable 'something' about his bowling, and that he was able to put a special 'devil' in the ball, not quite so pronounced in Walker. But Walker had one outstanding asset: his fielding to his own bowling was quite unequalled, whereas Clarke's was barely moderate. Lively fielding to one's own bowling is vitally important in an underarm bowler. Walker's eagerness to follow up the ball meant that he was often meeting almost face to face with batsmen who in his day were prepared to come out and attack him, but Walker showed complete fearlessness.

Inevitably, Clarke's success produced a number of bowlers who mistakenly believed that they too could revive the old style of bowling. The editor of *Scores and Biographies* stated that in about 1850, "many cricketers took to copying W. Clarke's slow underhand, some however with very poor success as to regularity of pitch. This kind of bowling (even if bad) often 'pays'; many crack batsmen who can beat off good round-arms are 'stuck up' when opposed to lobs." At about the same time James Pycroft in his book *The Cricket Field* (1851) showed that he was a supporter of the old-fashioned lobbing: "It is a valuable change in most elevens. A lobbing bowler with the long-stop and four men in all on the on-side will shorten the innings of many a reputed fine hitter." Later, in *Cricketana* (1865) Pycroft is having a moan about the shortage of good bowlers generally: "What then is to be done? . . . under-hand bowling appears in every match, and generally very bad under-hand bowling it is. For the most part it succeeds, if at all, because bowling that is bad is always apt to betray a man into batting that is worse."

Pycroft's reason for the low quality of the bowling is that "nearly all the present underhand bowlers pretend to what they never originally learnt to do." Walker is exempt from this complaint as he adopted the style when young. Tinley is the next bowler, but for all his recent practice, he had 'taken the hint' from the success of Clarke, and hasn't the advantage of being thoroughbred. Others including the leading batsman George Parr had taken up under-arm bowling late in life, and Pycroft felt that really skilful under-arm bowling can be achieved only after years of experience. The great batsman Bob Carpenter also took to bowling lobs. Copy-cat bowling seemed to Pycroft to be spurious.

This is the first mention of Robert Crispin Tinley. Born in 1830 he first played for Nottinghamshire as a teenager, and often caused the England XI many problems as a 'given' fast bowler, but like others he decided to alter his style and took up under-arm bowling in the late 1850s; he soon became rated as second only to Walker. H.S. Altham, in his classic book, regarded Tinley as "one of the best lob bowlers in cricket history". He delivered the ball hip-high and at a fair pace, and was able to produced considerable bias. When operating together with John Jackson the attack was said to have consisted of "a corkscrew at one end and a thunderbolt at the other". He must have been full of cunning and George Parr called him "the Spider", since he seemed to lure his victims into his web. In one match an officer who had endured the perils of the Charge of the Light Brigade was reduced to nervous impotence at the mere sight of Tinley's approach, and was out immediately. That Tinley managed to learn such art and accuracy in so short a time says much for a great natural talent. Among his skills he developed a ball delivered a yard behind the crease. Like many good lob bowlers he was devastating in matches against odds, and when he went on tour to North America with George Parr in 1863/64 he is said to have taken 250 wickets in 33 matches.

Tinley also excelled himself in the match between the England XI and XVIII of Hallam at Hyde Park, Sheffield in 1860. After taking 10 wickets in the first innings, bowling unchanged with Jackson, he then took all 17 wickets in the second innings, bowling unchanged and conceding only 58 runs. His full match figures read:- 208 balls, 112 runs, and 27 wickets. *Scores and Biographies* commented that the dead ground in that wet season was helpful to his slow lobs.

Tinley's fellow players had a high regard for his bowling. Here is Richard Daft's opinion: "R.C. Tinley was an underhand bowler whom I played with regularly for many years, and from whom I learnt a great deal as to how to play against lobs. Tinley was able to make the ball 'talk' almost when the wicket helped him: was as quick and as active as a kitten to field his own bowling, and was also, like Ulysses, 'full of wiles'. Another thing, no man, I believe, ever so fully realised how lobs should be played, and how they should not be played, as Tinley did. As regards my own batting performances against them he once paid me a great compliment."

Writing some ten years later in 1902, Alfred Shaw in his book of reminiscences paid Tinley even greater tribute: "I cannot close this chapter without making reference to that much neglected art, lob bowling. There is no one, in my opinion at the present day who can in the least be compared with my poor old friend, the late R. C. Tinley, as an under-hand bowler. I have never seen his equal. He had a remarkably true pitch, and he stood straight up and delivered the ball as high as the hip, unlike modern lob bowlers who generally crouch at the delivery and that in an ungainly fashion. Tinley too had what I supposed must be considered the rare gift of being able to vary his pace without lobbing the ball high in the air, while some of his deliveries would come off the ground as smartly as those of a good medium-pace bowler. He was in my opinion far in front of Mr V.E. Walker, Roger Iddison and Mr F. Townsend - all very good under-hand bowlers, and also Mr E.M. Grace, A.W. Ridley, and Walter Humphreys, who had each a good ball from the off-side. The reason is that Tinley gave the batsman no time to step out to his lobs and treat them as he pleased".

Tinley is mentioned in Prowse's famous *In Memoriam* poem on Alfred Mynn (1861) as "Tinley's slows are often telling, though they sometimes catch it hot."

Of those just recorded, Iddison had the satisfaction of clean bowling W.G. Grace after he had scored 101 for MCC *v* Yorkshire in 1872. There are other such dismissals by a lob bowler; Tinley bowled W.G. out in 1863, as also did I.D. Walker when he had scored 94 *v* Middlesex in 1884, and Humphreys caused him to hit his wicket after scoring 215 *v* Sussex in 1888.

W. G. himself tells the story of how the eccentric Tom Emmett was in 1878 out to one of Frank Townsend's 'curly underhand slows'. Emmett showed studied caution in allowing several of them to pass by, and then, again with uplifted bat, to his great annoyance, saw one of these twisters break sharply in and bowl him.

Apart from those lob bowlers already mentioned there were many others whose bowling was regarded as very successful, and *Scores and Biographies* recalls several of mid-Victorian times. In 1848 T.Rose bowled fast lobs for the England XI against XXII of Coventry, and a year later J.G. Nash for the Gentlemen of England *v* the Gentlemen of Kent at Canterbury was bowling "as almost the only slow under-hand bowler who (apart from Clarke) appears now in any match of note."

In 1852 V. Tinley, brother of 'R.C.' was playing for Devonshire *v* the England XI and "Bowling à la Clarke with good twist." A. Merchant and T.C. Goodrich, of the Free Foresters, are others named as excellent under-arm bowlers. The 1860s produced James Round (Oxford University, 1864) who kept wicket for the Gentlemen at Lord's but also at times bowled under-arm. No doubt most of these in their efforts at tempting deception delivered what was once referred to as a gentle tossed up 'popty' ball - a delightfully descriptive epithet.

Chapter 3

Clarke's Successors

William Clarke's success must have cheered the traditionalists who were feeling that the modern 'throwing' bowling had killed the lob for ever. As we have heard, according to Pycroft, several players switched to under-hand late in life, and sometimes did well enough with it. He believed however that a true lob bowler must learn his craft early, and he would have approved of at least one of Clarke's contemporaries, namely E.T. Drake. Educated at Westminster School, he won a Blue at Cambridge for three seasons, 1852-54, and though he played no county cricket, he appeared for the Gentlemen *v* Players at Lord's for 5 consecutive years, a very good record for one who was not a regular player. He entered the Church in 1860, and played little cricket afterwards, being one of many who were lost to cricket by their vocation. In his short career he took 197 first-class wickets, 20 times taking 5 wickets in an innings, and 8 times 10 wickets in a match; his best innings analysis was 8-61.

Drake is frequently listed among the more famous lob bowlers; we are told by Richard Daft that his delivery was lower than V.E. Walker's, producing a slow ball 'twisting in from the leg'. *Scores and Biographies* said that Drake's lobs "are at times very telling, but they receive a good deal of punishment. As a batsman, using a bat of great weight, he is one of the most slashing that has yet appeared, hitting at almost everything."

There were two other amateur bowlers who flitted briefly across the scene, but obviously possessed considerable talent. One was W.B. Money (1848-1924) who was educated at Harrow, and played for Cambridge University in 1868-71. As a schoolboy he had made his first-class dèbut for the Gentlemen of Kent in 1866 as a slow under-arm bowler who bowled left-handed, which was unusual. When at Harrow he had done the hat-trick *v* Eton in 1866. He was very successful in

University matches with figures of 5-29 *v* Oxford in 1868, and 6-24 and 5-35 (as opening bowler) in the following year. In all three Varsity matches he was a leading batsman, played for the Gentlemen at Lord's in 1869, and next year scored 70 and 109* for them in the Oval match. He entered the Church in 1871, and that was the end of his career at the age of 23 - yet another talented cricketer lost to the first-class game. Canon McCormick, who saw all the great lob bowlers from Clarke to Humphreys considered that V.E. Walker and Money were nearer each other in style than any two bowlers of the time; "Neither of them tossed the ball in the air as much as other bowlers such as A.W. Ridley or E.T. Drake . . . I never think Money had full justice done to him."

Another bowler, with an even briefer career, but obviously possessing much talent, was W.M. Rose (1842-1917). He first made his name when playing for North *v* South in the Canterbury week of 1871, where he routed the South with figures of 4 - 9 and 8 - 71, and in the next match of the week he followed this with 3 - 47 and 5 - 52 for MCC *v* Kent. That was virtually the end of his career, which covered only 7 matches with the capturing of 23 wickets. In a minor tour to America however in 1872, when bowling against XXII of Montreal he took 15 wickets in the first innings, and in the second he took all 19 wickets that fell to bowlers (there were 2 run outs). His match bag was therefore 34 wickets - a notable feat even against inferior opposition. C.I. Thornton considered E.M. Grace, Walter Humphreys and Rose to be the best lob bowlers he had ever seen.

Now for some of those who successfully took up lob bowling late in life. The best batsman of the day, George Parr (1826-91), adopted under-hand bowling and obtained 29 wickets in his career. The redoubtable John Wisden (1826-1884) decided in about 1857 to slow his pace down, and from time to time indulged in slow lob deliveries, though it is impossible to know just how many wickets he captured with these. Another contemporary, George (Ben) Griffith (1823-1879), took 670 wickets in his career, mostly for Surrey. He was also one of the best hitters of his time, and it is said that in about 1862 he took to bowling slow lobs. This made him one of the very few bowlers of left-handed lobs. W. B. Money has been mentioned, and others who come to mind were Nicholas Felix and H. Phillips. Felix's best bowling came in his single-wicket matches with Alfred Mynn in 1846.

Another to convert his style of bowling was William Mortlock (1832-1884). He played for Surrey chiefly as a middle order batsman, and was originally a medium pace bowler. When Surrey met Hampshire at the Oval 1865 they scored hugely with a total of 424, and then bowled out Hampshire for scores of 139 and 64. Mortlock bowled his lobs unchanged in both innings with figures of 5 - 66 and 3 - 35, and *Scores and Biographies* commented that "Mortlock's slow under-hand 'rubbish' again got wickets."

There was another group who indulged in lob bowling from time to time; these were wicket-keepers who wanted a little break from standing behind the stumps. The most interesting was C.H. Ellis of Sussex (1830-1880). He was primarily the Sussex wicket-keeper, but in the 80 matches of his career he also managed to capture 100 wickets. 1863 was his most successful season, when in a match against Surrey he not only scored 83, but took 15 wickets (8 - 96 and 7 - 201), and of these wickets no less than 6 were 'caught and bowled'. In the previous month, in a high scoring game against Kent at Hove, he had taken 9 wickets (7 - 73, including 3 in an over, and 2 - 59), scored 34 and 12, and in the Kent second innings he is also credited with 2 stumpings. He seems to have been a most genuine all-rounder.

A more freakish example of a wicket-keeper going on to bowl lobs was the performance of Tom Box (1808-1876). Sussex were playing England in 1849 and were having little success when "after the best bowlers had been beaten off", Box was called on to have a go and took 5 wickets for 45 runs, including those of Parr, Felix and Mynn - all clean bowled. The hilarity over this must have been considerable. Reports stated that Box got his wickets "by slow under hand lobs of the most ridiculous description, pitched anywhere and high in the air." Since Box took only three other wickets in his whole bowling career this performance must be regarded as the *locus classicus* of a very part-time lob bowler succeeding after the real bowlers had failed.

Tom Box's successor as the finest wicket-keeper of the day was Thomas Lockyer, of Surrey (1826-1869). He also used to indulge in some occasional bowling, usually with fastish round-armers, but sometimes with slow under-arm lobs; he was never more successful with these than against Kent at the Oval in 1862, where he had match-winning analyses of 3 - 11 and 6 - 33, all nine wickets taken in only 72 balls. He was assisted in the fall of some of his victims by H.H. Stephenson, an all-rounder, who could also keep wicket ably.

Also playing in this match was Edgar Willsher (1828-1885), the famous fast left-arm bowler from Kent, who, to quote *Scores and Biographies*, "delivered, for once, some under-hand balls." A few weeks later, again at the Oval, Willsher was concerned in a dramatic no-balling episode when John Lillywhite, the umpire, objected to him raising his arm illegally above the shoulder.

Several other distinguished wicket-keepers have sometimes left their post and indulged in a brief spell of lob bowling. E. Pooley (1838-1907) of Surrey took 6 wickets in a career of 370 matches; George Pinder of Yorkshire (1841-1903) took 23 wickets at the low cost of 20.91 runs each, with a best analysis of 4 - 56, and it is said that he "usually bowled with his pads on", thereby ignoring the risk of being penalised for 5 runs if the ball had hit these pads. Harry Phillips (1844-1919) took 14 wickets (4-33 best analysis) with his rare left-handed lobs. J.McC. Blackham (1854-1932), the Australian wicket-keeper, in a career of 275 matches captured 2 wickets for 138 runs, probably those of G.S. Marriott (Oxford University) 'bowled' in 1878, and H.V. Page (Gloucestershire) 'lbw' in 1884. The story of the wicket-keeper Alfred Lyttelton's lobs in a Test Match will now be told; a most bizarre example of such bowling which attracted great attention, and has frequently been the subject of discussion.

August 11th, 1884 was the opening day of the last of a series of three Test matches between England and Australia. The first had been drawn and England had won the second. Winning the toss, Australia made the most of a good Oval wicket, and by the close of play had scored 363 - 2, with P.S. McDonnell, W.L. Murdoch and H.J.H. Scott all scoring hundreds. Towards the end of the day Lord Harris, the England captain, rested the regular bowlers and even asked the wicket-keeper, the Hon. Alfred Lyttelton, to take off his pads and bowl. A report says; "His bowling was very erratic, the ball generally going wide on the leg side." There is no evidence that he was bowling under-hand on this day. W.W. Read took his place behind the wicket, after himself bowling lobs for figures of 7 - 0 - 36 - 0 (4 balls to the over). One down in the series, Australia had every reason to go all out for a win, but with declarations not yet legally possible, the batsmen next day took every risk to hit or get out, but they batted on longer than the situation seemed to require. With the score at 532-6 Lord Harris again called on Lyttelton to bowl from the Vauxhall end, but this time he bowled under-hand, kept his pads on, and W.G. Grace went behind the stumps when he was bowling. This was confirmed by an eye-witness in H. Preston, who later became editor of *Wisden.*

With his very first lob ball Lyttelton had Midwinter caught at the wicket by W.G.; he next bowled Spofforth, had Boyle caught, and then Blackham lbw, for the side to be all out for 551. On this second day Lyttelton had taken 4 wickets for 8 runs in 8 overs, to end up with a final analysis of 12 - 5 - 19 - 4. His brother Edward Lyttelton believed that Alfred was helped by the batsmen's readiness to get out; towards the very end of the innings Shrewsbury was also asked to bowl, possibly because it amused Lord Harris to call on every member of the side to bowl. Harris himself wrote; "At last, having exhausted the wiles of the regular bowlers I resorted to giving everyone a turn, and so hit on the key to the position in Alfred Lyttelton, with his pads on, with lobs." W.G. said that Lyttelton's lobs were 'very bad'; the lbw was off a long-hop, one bounced three times, and another went like a snail.

At the end of the second day (only 3 days were then allotted to Test matches) England had scored 181 - 8, and were in some danger of defeat, but W.W. Read, going in unusually late at number 10, scored a dashing 117, the total reached 346 and the game ended in a draw. In the whole of his first class career from 1876 to 1897 Alfred Lyttelton is listed as having taken 4 wickets for 172 runs. There is no evidence of his having bowled lobs except on the second day of the Test Match, and brother Edward in a letter to *The Times* in 1937 said; "So far as I know Alfred had never bowled a lob before", and it seems that after this he never bowled a lob again. When once asked, he jokingly replied that after his Test Match success he decided to retire from bowling.

Enough of such frivolity. By the 1870s the big names in under-hand bowling had departed, and in the following decade only one top-class lob bowler came to the fore. This was A.W. (Jammy) Ridley (1852-1916). Educated at Eton, he won a blue at Oxford for 4 seasons, 1872-1875, and it was in his last season as captain that he rekindled the reputation of lobs. In the previous season he had as an opening bowler taken 7 Cambridge wickets, and of these five were bowled, one caught and bowled, and the other stumped. In 1875 Cambridge wanted 174 to win. They had reached 161 - 7 when it is said that W.H. Game persuaded his captain to go on with his lobs. Let Ridley tell the story himself:

"I went on to bowl much against my judgement. My first ball got rid of W.H. Patterson, then Macan came in and made a single off the next. This brought Sims to my end, and he hit my third ball clean over my head for four, and afterwards made it 7 to win. It was now that Sims was caught, and Arthur Smith came in. He looked rather shaky and no wonder. He managed to keep his wicket intact for two balls, but my third bowled him, amid terrific excitement, so Oxford

24

won by 6 runs." Edward Lyttelton stated that the ball with which the victorious lob bowler dismissed each of his victims was "a straight low one on the leg stump, which did not turn an inch."

This dramatic finish was fully reported, since in those days the Varsity match attracted huge crowds. Another Lyttelton, the Hon. R.H., recalls how "Sims with a mighty smack sent a ball from Ridley like a cannon shot to the ropes. Mr Smith now had the crisis he had been dreading - the air was chilly, the ground was wet, and the sun invisible. He somehow or other stopped two balls in a doubtful sort of way, and played slowly forward to the third, thinking that after the manner of lobs it would twist. The wet ground prevented this; it went on and hit the middle stump, and Oxford had won."

Ridley's action in putting himself on was regarded as one "of quite remarkable courage", and at the end "he was the only person at Lord's ground whose calmness was entirely undisturbed by this dramatic finish". His final analysis of 4.3 - 0 - 16 - 2 may not look anything special but it proved that lob bowling could still achieve unexpected success, especially when the opposing side was under stress.

There is no doubt that Ridley was a very good bowler, and David Frith noted that he was unlucky not to have won an England cap when Test cricket began a few years later.

Another comment concerning Ridley can be found in *The Walkers of Southgate*:- "R.D. Walker (one of the famous brotherhood) had a supreme contempt for underhand slow bowlers. He once told Jammy Ridley that he thought he might bowl to him all the week without getting him out, and he added, "I fancy Ridley was not inclined to disagree". Ridley was almost the last of the great amateur lob bowlers until the coming of Jephson some twenty years later. He was also a batsman good enough to score a century at Lord's against the Players in 1876, and like most lob bowlers he was a brilliant field to his own bowling, and followed the ball right down the wicket.

There was one other contemporary lob bowler of a very different kind. The under-arm bowling of E.M. Grace (1841-1911) came about almost by accident. Originally he bowled fast round-arm, but in a club match for Lansdown *v* South Wilts in 1861, to quote his own words, "We couldn't get the South Wilts men out, and at length the captain came up to me and said; 'Do you think you could manage to bowl a few lobs?' I said, 'Oh, yes, it's all the same to me', so I went on and much to my surprise took seven wickets in each innings. (His figures were in fact 7 - 60 and 4 - 36). I had, of course, like everybody else, occasionally bowled lobs at practice for fun, but I had never dreamed of doing so in a match." (His younger brother, W.G., also stated that E.M. had often bowled lobs at home.)

This was the start of E.M. Grace's career as a lob bowler. In the course of his first-class career he took 305 wickets and many of these were with lobs, though he varied his bowling style with the odd round-arm ball, and sometimes very high tossed up balls intended to land on top of the bails. His first-class debut was in 1862, when after many fine performances in minor cricket he was invited to play for England against XIV of Kent in the Canterbury week. He scored 0 (out first ball) in the first innings, and then top-scored with 56 in the second, though again he should have been out first ball. His analysis was 0-22. He was then requested to play in the next match as a guest for MCC against the Gentlemen of Kent (12 a-side). Some protest was made that he was not then a member of MCC but he played nonetheless. When the Gentlemen batted first and were all out for 141 Grace took 5 wickets. MCC then made 344, of which, going in first and batting through the innings, Grace made no less than 192*. Boundary hits for four were allowed in this game and he hit 26 of them. To follow this he then took all ten wickets that fell in Kent's second innings, since one man was absent. His figures were 32.2 - 7 - 69 - 10. Even though the opposition was not very powerful this represents one of the finest all-round cricketing feats ever recorded in cricket history. Most of the wickets were taken with slow under-hand balls, but he sometimes put in an unexpected round-arm which took the batsman by surprise. It would not have been necessary to inform him of any such change of action.

Grace's lob bowling had plenty of variation in height, pace and spin. To quote his biographer, F.S. Ashley-Cooper, "Many batsmen hated his bowling and were greatly relieved when he was taken off." C.I. Thornton said that he kept his hand very close to the ground, but the ball did not rise high in the air in the way it did with many lob bowlers; on one occasion however the ball did rise very high. This was when he was playing for XVIII Gentlemen of Surrey *v* The United South of England XI at the Oval in September 1865.

H. Jupp (of the South) was always hard to dismiss, and E.M. Grace, who made top scores of 56 and 64, went on with high tosses. The first ball was lobbed up about 15 yards high, and Jupp hit it for 2; the second, higher still, deceived the batsman, and alighted on the stumps, removing the bails, "H. Jupp, bowled Grace,

22". Whereupon there were howls of protest from the crowd, who invaded the pitch. The report reads; "The Little Doctor stood on the pitch, stump in hand, and remarked to the angry crowd surrounding him that the first man who touched him would get the middle stump on his head - and he meant it. The game could not be continued for about three-quarters of an hour, and then, nothing daunted, E.M.G. continued his 'shell practice'." The United were easily defeated and Grace with analyses of 6 - 78 and 7 - 65 bowled unchanged through the two innings with I.D. Walker, another lob bowler.

Another fine performance with lobs was to take 3 - 17 and 6 - 36 v Surrey at the Oval in 1871. He went on playing in club cricket for many years after his county days were over - right up to 1909 - and he took masses of wickets, the total helped perhaps by his frequently being captain of the side. He would continue to bowl however much he was hit about; it was the wickets that mattered, not the cost. The most savage treatment he suffered was from W. Hyman, playing for Bath Association v Thornbury at Thornbury in July 1902. Hyman scored 359* in 100 minutes, out of a total of 461 - 6. He took 62 runs off two consecutive overs from Grace - 666446, 666444 - but Grace remained unperturbed as he bowled from one end throughout the innings. On another occasion when Newport scored 482 v Thornbury, on July 28 1904, Grace also bowled unchanged for an analysis of 35.2 - 1 - 320 - 5.

In 1884 Grace had a famous meeting with George Bonnor, the giant Australian hitter. When Bonnor came in, E.M. went up to W.G. and said, "I can get him out quicker than anyone". W.G. was doubtful, but said, "Well then, but only two overs." Bonnor chimed in with "Are you going on, Doctor?" "Yes," said E.M., "and I'm going to get you out." As was permitted in those days, E.M. bowled about a dozen trial balls to the wicket-keeper, some round-arm, some under-arm. Bonnor then took his guard; "What sort are you going to bowl, Doctor?"; "You'll see soon enough", was the reply. The first ball was a slow under-arm, and Bonnor, now totally bemused, popped it gently up to W.G. at point. "I told you so," said E.M. It was a perfect example of his impudent approach to batsmen.

No cricketer has ever played the game with more energy, enterprise and courage. In his fielding at point, it was said he would start a yard from the bat, and then creep in; he would take the hardest slash made at him with complete composure. If E.M. had not later been overshadowed by his seven years younger brother, he would have been acknowledged as the greatest cricketer of the age. He had every quality of an all-round cricketer, and an overwhelming personality. How the media of today would have welcomed him.

A few more bowlers of that time must be mentioned. One was I.D.Walker (1844-1898), who was the youngest of the famous brotherhood. Here is an account of his bowling by A.J.Webbe, who was himself most skilled in playing lobs. In about 1900 he wrote;

"As a bowler, Walker suited his style to the batsmen, very few of whom ever got to the ball before it pitched. His lobs were never slow, and occasionally he bowled very fast for over after over - not daisy-cutters but good-pitched balls. He varied his pace a great deal, had a good twist from leg, and fielded his own bowling well. But unlike the present-day lob bowler, he hardly bowled on the leg-side at all, but rather pitched the ball on the middle and off stumps. As a rule he placed his field as if for slow round-arm bowling."

W.A.Bettesworth adds that he was not unlike his brother V.E. in method and style. It was as a batsman that I.D.Walker was chiefly famous, and he was the best of the six brothers. To quote A.J.Webbe again: "He was a magnificent bat, and he had one remarkable stroke that sent the ball high over the heads of point or cover. It seemed as if he was facing cover point and making straight drives. He would often come in without pads or gloves and attack the bowling from the start."

Next comes a rarity in underarm bowlers in that he was a professional. Thomas Armitage (1848-1922) played for Yorkshire and in a short career between 1872-1879 he took 119 wickets, in his latter years mostly by lobs. In 1875, playing against Nottinghamshire at Trent Bridge, 5 wickets had fallen for 47 when, to quote *Lillywhite*, "The Yorkshire captain Rowbotham thought of Armitage's lobs. It was a happy notion, for Notts rushed out madly to meet the slows and Pinder stumped four of the remaining batsmen". Nottinghamshire were all out for 58, and Armitage's figures were 17 balls - 8 runs - 5 wickets. It was a fine example of how the very sight of lobs can create a frenzy with disastrous results.

In the following season, against Surrey at Sheffield, Armitage was not only top scorer with 47 out of the Yorkshire score of 173, but he produced two analyses of 67 balls - 20 runs - 6 wickets, and 70 balls - 26 runs - 7 wickets to rout Surrey for totals of 74 and 41. *Lillywhite* commented that Armitage's lobs "could scarcely have been played worse by infants", but his figures of 13 - 46 in the match are among the best ever achieved by a lob bowler. In 1877 he again routed Surrey at Sheffield with second innings figures of 31.2 - 12 - 58 - 7, and a few weeks later at the Oval he again dismayed them with an analysis of 10 - 7 - 8 - 5, but reports suggest that this time he may have been bowling some slow round-arm balls mixed in with his lobs.

Armitage went with James Lillywhite on the pioneer tour to Australia in 1876-7, and played in both Test matches. On the opening day of the first match the close-of-play score was "Australia 166 - 6, A. C. Bannerman 126*". With the total at 100 - 3, Armitage was put on to bowl, and immediately sent a full toss right over Bannerman's head - "to be reached only by a clothes' prop" - as one critic wrote. He then resorted to grubbers. The crowd was shaking with laughter, as nothing like this had been see in the colonies before, but Bannerman liked it and scored from almost every ball. After three unsuccessful overs for 15 runs, Armitage was taken off.

Another very occasional under-hand bowler was Richard Daft (1835-1900) who in the 1870s was regarded as the best professional batsman in England, with a beautiful easy style. In the course of a long career, he took 51 wickets, mostly with slow lobs. One good day was against Surrey at the Oval in 1869, when the home side, coasting smoothly along to a draw, lost their last 5 wickets for 10 runs to be all out for 208. Daft took four of these wickets for 0 runs in the course of 10 balls - all stumpings by Biddulph - and turned the game towards victory. His final analysis was 5 - 23 in the course of 14 (4 ball) overs. On another occasion he went even better with figures of 6 - 59.

This selection of the more distinguished lob bowlers of the day gives little idea of the frequency with which lob bowlers were seen in action in big cricket. Fortunately there is some evidence given in *Lillywhite's Annual* for 1871 to 1876 where figures are provided of all bowlers who took at least one wicket in a season and, most helpfully, a note is added of their mode of bowling, e.g. 'lobs'.

Of the 19 lob bowlers listed, 'Willis' (Sgt. W. McCanlis), Iddison, Gilby, Charlwood, Phillips, Pooley, and Armitage were professionals. The average bag for the season was 75 wickets, but this figure is largely boosted by the success of A.W. Ridley. Several of those listed have already been discussed, and it seems worthwhile to add something about others who did not appear much on the *Lillywhite* list for these years.

Bowler	1871	1872	1873	1874	1875
F.F.J. Greenfield	-	-	-	-	21
E.M. Grace	24	8	14	-	-
R. Daft	8	15	2	-	-
W.M. Rose	21	-	-	-	-
W.B. Money	3	-	-	-	-
'Willis'	3	-	3	-	-
F. Townsend	4	-	2	-	6
R. Iddison	6	12	2	-	-
I.D. Walker	1	6	20	8	12
A.W. Ridley	-	30	26	23	38
W. Gilby	-	2	-	-	-
F.R. Reynolds	-	-	2	-	-
W. Coppinger	-	-	7	-	-
J.H. Ponsonby	-	-	2	6	4
H.R.J. Charlwood	-	-	1	-	-
C.S. Gordon	-	-	-	3	-
H. Phillips	-	-	-	5	-
E. Pooley	-	-	-	3	-
T. Armitage	-	-	-	-	10

F R. Reynolds of Lancashire was once a fast round-arm bowler, who later turned to slow lobs, some of which must have been responsible for the 200 wickets he took in his career. Roger Iddison who took over 250 wickets for Yorkshire (and later Lancashire) was another who changed to under-arm bowling; it was said that his bowling was so slow that he could run after the ball and fetch it back if it was not satisfactory. He toured Australia in 1861-2. Sgt. W. McCanlis, who appeared for Kent under the name 'Willis', took 18 wickets in his career. J.H. Ponsonby (later Ponsonby-Fane), a nephew of Lord Bessborough, took 13 wickets in a brief career for MCC. F. Townsend, the father of 'C.L.' and of 'A.F.M.' (who also bowled lobs) took 101 wickets for Gloucestershire.

F.P.U. Pickering, Oxford University and Sussex, bowled fast under-arm in successfully taking 8 wickets for 64 in his brief career. W. Gilby played in one match for Middlesex in 1872 and took 2 wickets. C.S. Gordon played for Victoria and Gloucestershire in 14 matches with 8 wickets; underarm bowling overseas seems to have been very rare.

W. Coppinger played in 7 matches for Kent between 1868 and 1873. F.G. Monkland, an old Reptonian, played in 26 matches for Gloucestershire without taking a wicket. H.R.J. Charlwood, a very successful Sussex batsman who played for England in the two pioneer Test matches of 1876-7, also bowled the occasional lob.

Another, more successful, of a later decade was E. Sainsbury, of Somerset and Gloucestershire, who took 25 wickets with his lobs in 46 matches. A.N. Hornby was said to have bowled with either hand, but took only 11 wickets in a lengthy career. One of these was at Sheffield in 1881 when he had Tom Emmett stumped off his second under-hand ball.

Lob bowling at this time was sufficiently rare for *Baily's Magazine* of July 1873 to make the comment on a match between Gents of the South and Players of the North at Prince's; "We had the singular spectacle at one part of the game of an under-hand bowler at each end in a first-class match - a circumstance almost unprecedented since the introduction of round-arm bowling". (The bowlers were Ridley and E.M. Grace.) There was another such oddity in 1886 when a pioneer team of Parsees met the MCC at Lord's in a match not of first-class status. On being put into bat, W.G. Grace and I.D. Walker put on 119 for the first wicket and each of the two Parsee opening bowlers was bowling under-hand. When the visitors batted they were all out for 23 and 66, being quite unable to cope with I.D. Walker's lobs, backed up by Grace's cunning slow round-arms.

In his book *The Game of Cricket* (1887) Frederick Gale made the comment that lob bowling seemed to be lacking in really skilled performers and he wrote this pleasant piece of advice for those called upon 'to pitch a lob'; "It is very amusing when a match is getting desperate and an 'emergency' slow lob bowler is put on as a last resource, to see the extraordinary useless antics of some slow bowlers. You see a man sometimes, who is sane and rational in ordinary life and a fair cricketer perhaps, who suddenly, on being asked to bowl lobs, goes off his head, and because he is asked to bowl an over of slows, extemporises a kind of double cut and shuffle hornpipe step, shakes his hand up and down as if he were rattling a dice-box, then turns an imaginary organ handle, and produces as the result a very one-horse-slow, on-leg, long-hop which goes over the boundary for four. All the preliminary antics in the world will not put any 'devil' into slows, any more than cushion-thumping can put sense into a stupid sermon."

Another source of information about lob bowlers of earlier days is the invaluable *Who's Who of Cricketers* (Bailey, Thorn and Wynne-Thomas, 1984). This covers all those who have appeared in first-class-cricket. Between 1860 and 1900 the authors note nearly 50 players (in addition to those already mentioned) as bowlers of under-arm or lobs, spread evenly over the period, but few of them had much success.

The matter is complicated by some bowlers being designated for example as "fast right-hand, later under-arm", which makes any wickets taken with under-arm deliveries impossible to identify. Some, like others already mentioned, were wicket-keepers ready to bowl the occasional lob. Only three, I.D. Walker, F.P.U. Pickering and R. Brotherhood were named as 'fast under-arm'. There were one or two oddities; W. Yardley is said to have bowled fast with his right-hand over-arms, and slow with his under-arm left-handers, and the two Mordaunts, "G.J." and "O.", used either hand to bowl lobs, but took no wickets.

Chapter 4

The Magnificent Swan-Song: Humphreys, Jephson & Simpson-Hayward

The coming of the 1890s brought little suggestion that there might be any revival of the lob. County cricket was soon to be extended and more organised, and less likely to indulge in old-fashioned methods. There had been a flicker of excitement when in a festival match at Scarborough in 1891 W.W. Read had achieved an analysis of 6 - 24, which included one of the rare under-arm 'hat-tricks'. He had been among the best batsmen in England and, though originally a fast bowler, had taken up lob bowling with some success. We have met his lobs before in that historic Oval Test match of 1884.

Among Read's victims was J. Briggs who in 1885 was stumped off one of his 'under-hand twisters' after scoring 186. In a later season Briggs was again dismissed by Read with a very odd ball; "It did not seem to rise more than two feet above the ground and it seemed it might not reach the wicket. Briggs tried to block it, but it rolled round him with just enough force to break the wicket." *The Manchester Guardian* described the delivery as 'the sort of ball a boy of eight or nine sends down. It was absolutely ludicrous to see the daisy cutter roll into the wicket without the astounded batsman making any attempt to prevent it."

Read was involved in an entertaining incident in 1893 when Middlesex met Surrey at Lord's. Sir Timothy O'Brien was batting well and in order to induce a catch Read went on to bowl his lobs down the leg-side to a packed field. O'Brien realised that the lobs were not breaking so he decided to turn round completely and just as the ball was passing clear of the leg-stump to drive it with terrific force behind him to the pavilion rails. Wood, the wicket-keeper, was terrified and ran for refuge into the slips. In attempting a fifth such boundary, O'Brien hit the ground instead of the ball, a cloud of dust came up, and then the off-bail was seen lying on the ground. The wicket-keeper claimed that O'Brien had trodden on his wicket. O'Brien said that Wood had disturbed it, and the umpires both said they were unsighted. O'Brien stated firmly, "I'm not going anyhow", and went on to score 113.

In the season of 1892 there was some mild interest in the news that Oxford University were to include a lob bowler against Cambridge. Could he, like Ridley, produce another dramatic result? His name was J.B. Wood (1870-1933). He had come from Marlborough, and, after scoring 61 in the Seniors match, played one game for the University in 1891, purely as a batsman. The following year he again scored well for the Seniors with an innings of 72, but it was only after some outstanding bowling with lobs in college matches that the Oxford captain, L.C.H. Palairet, decided to give him a trial. He had instant success against Lancashire with an analysis of 5 - 33; he continued to do well and was granted his Blue.

After Oxford had scored 365, Cambridge had to bat for a short spell in the evening during which they lost their No. 1 batsman, R.N. Douglas, clean bowled for 2 by Wood, who was one of the opening bowlers. It had been a long time at Lord's since a lob bowler was seen going on first in a big match, and for many spectators lob bowling was a rare experience. Cambridge were clearly mesmerised by this strange form of attack and thanks also to some suicidal run outs they were all out for 160. They had previously heard about Wood's lobs and allowed themselves to imagine all sorts of difficulties, though *The Cricket Field* had reported that there was nothing very dangerous about him since, "his slow lobs were too slow to be effective against a resolute bat on a hard wicket". F.S. Jackson had played him with ease.

Cambridge recovered in their second innings to make a better game of it but lost in the end by 5 wickets; Wood took 4 more wickets, but was expensive. His match figures of 3 - 53 (all bowled) and 4 - 120 may not seem devastating, but his mere presence among the Oxford bowlers had created a feeling of uncertainty in the enemy camp. Wood continued to bowl well in 1893, taking 5 - 56 *v* Lancashire, and 6 - 68 against the Gentlemen of England, but though he again opened the bowling in the University match he took only one wicket, and that was really the end of his career as he didn't go on to play county cricket. In his brief career he took 53 wickets for 26.93 runs each; this may sound expensive, but the names of some of his victims are impressive, including Sugg, Briggs (twice), W. Newham, Bean (twice), G. Brann (bowled for 0), G.F. Vernon, W.L. Murdoch (twice), R. Douglas, L.H. Gay, the big hitter H.T. Hewett (twice), S.M.J. Woods, Lord Hawke, and F.S. Jackson - a very fine collection for a bowler whom 'Country Vicar' described as 'indifferent'. His success lay in the very fact that he was 'different'.

The Cricket Field, in a long editorial, hoped that Wood's success might lead to some revival of lob bowling - "Several county teams use a lob bowler when they are 'tied up', but only one, Sussex, in Walter Humphreys, use a lob bowler as chief weapon." Humphreys was about to blossom; here is his strange story.

Walter ('Punter') Humphreys (1849-1924) made his first appearance for Sussex in 1871, scoring 44 on his debut. He was hailed in *Lillywhite's* notes as "a painstaking sound young batsman of whom great things are expected". After this good start, he had by the end of his seventh season (1877), played only 57 innings for Sussex with a moderate average of 16.04. He had also bowled 40 balls without success for 42 runs. He was probably not bowling lobs, and was mentioned as being able to keep wicket usefully. He made no appearances for Sussex in 1878 or 1879, and it seemed that his career was over, since he was already aged over 30. He could now spend more time on his business as a cobbler.

During these two blank seasons, however, he took up bowling lobs for his club, Brighton Brunswick, where he is said to have come under the guidance of P.G.H. Fender's grandfather who was a keen exponent of under-arm bowling. Humphreys' new skill with lobs in club cricket suggested to the Sussex Committee that it might be worth having him back for a trial, so in mid-August 1880 he made a reappearance, playing in four matches. His success as a bowler was very slight until the game against the Australians. In their innings of 154, he captured 5 wickets for 32 including those of T.U. Groube (bowled), Blackham (caught and bowled) and Bonnor, who put up a simple catch - all these wickets in the course of three balls, though the cricket report does not mention the term 'hat-trick'. The only other lob bowlers to achieve this rare feat were William Clarke, W.W. Read, and D.L.A. Jephson.

In spite of this achievement Humphreys played in only four games in 1881, taking a mere 4 wickets for 179 runs. In 1882, however, he was recalled and was taking just enough wickets to keep his place in a side that was short of bowling.

Over the 10 seasons 1882 - 1891 he averaged 36 wickets a year, with 57 his best bag in 1884, in which season he again triumphed against the Australian tourists with analyses of 6 - 97 and 5 - 69, including a hat-trick in the second innings, his victims this time being P.S. McDonnell, G. Giffen and H.J.H. Scott. He was to have yet another success against the Australians in 1888, when in their defeat he had figures of 9.3 - 2 - 21 - 5 and 9 - 2 - 19 - 4, thus taking 9 wickets in only 75 balls. In 1893 he again puzzled them with an analysis of 6 - 49. This success against the tourists was quite remarkable; they never seemed to take his bowling seriously and were clearly baffled by it.

There were other match-winning feats over this period. In 1883, at Sheffield, Yorkshire seemed to be heading for victory, and at lunch with 3 wickets left they needed only 17 runs to win; this was soon reduced to only 8 runs but Humphreys took these vital wickets for Sussex to be victorious by 3 runs. This was yet another example of how a lob bowler can win success in moments of tension. In 1893 there was a similar example; Gloucestershire were sensing victory when the Sussex captain, W. L. Murdoch, put Humphreys on to bowl. As he took the ball he heard a cry from the crowd; "Humphreys going on! Well, we might as well chuck it up!", but Humphreys then took 7 wickets for 30, including bowling the dangerous E.M. Grace for 0. Gloucestershire were all out for 196 and Sussex had again won by 3 runs.

Though *Wisden,* in its report on the Sussex season of 1889, had regarded Humphreys as "one of the most individual cricketers, but as a player, as an old man", but agreed that his unusual bowling gave some variety to the weak Sussex attack. No one, however, was prepared for this "old man's" remarkable advance in 1892, when he took 92 wickets for Sussex, and he went even better in 1893 with 150 wickets, of which 122 came in county games, surpassing the aggregate of 112 wickets taken by all the other bowlers. For a lob bowler to have to carry the attack to such an extent meant very hard work and it might be imagined that after such a long acquaintance with his bowling most county batsmen would have solved its secrets.

Apart from his feat against Gloucestershire just mentioned, in 1893 he had innings analyses of 8 - 98 *v* Yorkshire, 7 - 109 *v* Kent, 8 - 83 *v* Middlesex, as well as 15 wickets (7 - 72 and 8 -121) against Somerset. When Sussex arrived at Taunton for this last match Humphreys was greeted with the remark, "You won't be of much use today for Mr I.D. Walker has been giving the Somerset eleven

36

some practice in facing lobs." It does not seem to have done them much good. Humphreys' bag of 150 wickets in 1893 at the low cost of 17.48 runs was exceeded only by J.T. Hearne with 212 wickets, T. Richardson with 174, and Mold and Briggs with 166 each, so it made him the most successful slow right-hand bowler of the season.

One reason for such success lay in the astute handling of him by his captain W.L. Murdoch who brought him on to face every new batsman and used him in short but frequent spells. Another reason was that Butt, the wicket-keeper, grew more used to taking his bowling and missed fewer chances off him. It is not fully appreciated that lob bowling provided wicket keepers with peculiar difficulties, which resulted in many chances going astray.

In the following season of 1894 Humphreys was unable to repeat such performances and took only 36 wickets, his best effort being figures of 3 - 68 and 6 - 61 (the last five for 2 runs in 18 balls) v Somerset. In spite of this lack of form Humphreys was selected to tour Australia with Stoddart's team in the winter. No doubt his success against Australian touring teams had influenced the selectors, and it is alleged that the Melbourne Club had requested his selection. There was no problem about the veteran's fitness since he was a keen bicycle rider.

But it was a gamble that did not come off in the Test matches. According to A.C. MacLaren, a fellow team member, Humphreys was bowling as well as ever, but he took only six wickets for 314 runs in the first-class matches and did not appear in any Test. In the minor games he was devastating and in the overall tour figures he topped the list with 79 wickets at a cost of only 11.62 runs each. Inferior batsmen can seldom cope with lobs and tend to launch a frenzied but fruitless attack, but in the big matches the Australians played him very carefully and made his bowling innocuous. One memorable moment for him on this tour was carving the beef on Christmas day by reason of his seniority.

This tour virtually ended Humphreys' career. In 1895 he played in only three matches for Sussex and took only 13 wickets, and in the following season he played in only one game, but that was not quite the end of his long career, because in 1900 he moved back to Hampshire and played for that county in two matches. Though he took 8 wickets against Kent he decided that at the age of fifty it was time to retire. It was hoped that his son, Walter Humphreys, jun. (1878 - 1960) might follow in his father's footsteps as a lob bowler. He played in 14 matches for

Sussex between 1898 and 1900, but he took only 48 wickets at a high cost and was not retained. His best efforts were 5 - 107 and 3 - 59 *v* Hampshire in 1899.

In the course of his extraordinary career Walter Humphreys took 718 first-class wickets at a cost of 21.52 runs each which makes a record total for an under-arm bowler. In an interview with W.A. Bettesworth in 1894 he made some interesting comments on the nature of lob bowling:

"I can assure you that it is the hardest of hard work to bowl lobs. It may seem easy, but it is not. I put out all my strength when I am bowling, and a fast bowler can do no more. You see, I take a long run and follow up the ball a long way."

This follow-up sometimes put him in danger, and at Scarborough in 1893 he followed very close up when bowling to F.S. Jackson, who drove the ball very hard back at him and by one of those freaks of cricket it stuck; Jackson could hardly believe he was out. On another occasion he took an even harder 'caught and bowled' from the left-handed H.T. Hewett, whom Humphreys considered to be the most powerful hitter of the day. He said that he liked to bowl to hitters "because there is a considerable amount of excitement about it." He told Bettesworth that he preferred a fast wicket because "the ball goes on at once and does its work." His supreme skill lay in his power of disguising the break of the ball; when the Australian W. L. Murdoch (later to be his Sussex captain) scored 286* against Sussex in 1882 - an early date in Humphreys' bowling career - he stated that even when he had made 200 he could not tell from watching his hand which way he meant to turn the ball - a very high compliment.   S.M.J. Woods said that Humphreys was far and away the best lob bowler he ever saw or played against.

Sometimes those batsmen watching Humphreys' hand were distracted by the sleeve of his pink flannel shirt flapping in the breeze. He said that leaving the shirt unfastened was really a matter of habit as it was difficult to keep done up. There was no intention to distract the batsman, but after a few objections had been made to the flapping sleeve he made a special effort to fasten it, and bowled just as well. There is no doubt that with all slow bowlers - and especially lob ones - a considerable amount of cunning is needed. Humphreys was always annoyed with those who asked him how long it would take to learn to bowl 'that stuff'. "Would a week be long enough?" He replied indignantly -and he never suffered fools gladly - that his skill had taken him twenty years to learn and he was justifiably proud of it.

After the First World War Humphreys used to be seen at Hove sitting on the benches below what is now the secretary's office. He did not converse much with spectators, but one of them - then a schoolboy - recalls the thrill of speaking with him, his own hand completely enveloped in the huge soft hand of the veteran, who murmured something about it being good to see the young interested in cricket. Humphreys died in 1924 and that brought a reminder that the era of professional lob bowlers was over. A few other amateurs were to achieve fame but no professional was ever again to tackle such a precarious undertaking.

At the time of the height of Humphreys' success Richard Daft in his book *Kings of Cricket* (1893) suggested that others should follow his example and learn the business of lob bowling:

"Humphreys has been so successful with his lobs as to make one more convinced about the advisability of having a good under-hand bowler in all county teams. It is nearly always found that there is at least one man - generally several - in an eleven who cannot play lobs at all well, though they may be very good bats against round-arm bowling, and I would advise all young players, who are played for their batting, yet are not good bowlers, to practise bowling lobs, and I would advise any captain to try a lob bowler against any batsman who is difficult to get out."

A few years later K. S. Ranjitsinhji was to support Daft's suggestion. In his days with Sussex he knew all about Humphreys and fully discussed lob bowling when in a period of convalescence he put together what was to be called *The Jubilee Book of Cricket* (1897). He pointed out its qualities and possibilities:

"When runs are of no consequence and getting wickets is all-important, a lob bowler is a treasure. At the worst of times he is sure to be very useful as a change bowler, to be put on for an over or two. . . His great aim is to bowl balls which are difficult to score off unless hit in the air. I am convinced that most batsmen fall victims to lobs, not so much by the intrinsic difficulty and merit of the bowling, but on account of their own nervousness and anxiety to score. In matches where nerve plays an important part, even bad lobs are extraordinarily successful."

It is possibly surprising to find in an appreciation of Ranji's book that the poet Francis Thompson ("Oh my Hornby and my Barlow long ago!") made some very astute observations on the technique of lob bowling. He had noticed that a full pitch from an over-arm bowler formed a parabola, quite different from that delivered by an under-arm bowler. The full pitch from the latter has a much steeper fall, making it harder to judge, and pitching a ball well up is harder physically for the over-arm bowler, because of the ease and naturalness of the lob bowler's action. He also noted that the good-length ball, so vital for the over-arm bowler, was not so necessary for the lob bowler who had really more scope for varieties of bowling. What a pity Thompson did not write more about cricket.

That splendid bowler Alfred Shaw in his book of cricket reminiscences (1902) fully supported Ranji's views about under-arm bowling; "I am quite sure that all our counties would do well to have among their teams one good lob under-hand bowler. He should be a good batsman, of course, for obviously it would not pay to include a man in any team today for his lob bowling alone. I believe there are many first-class batsmen who would increase their usefulness to their side if they would learn to bowl slow under-hand."

Humphreys had gone and the cricket world was speculating on the final demise of all serious under-hand bowling, but the story was not over yet. D.L.A. Jephson (1871-1926) was given a trial in the Freshers match at Cambridge in 1890, and after doing well as a fast-medium bowler with an action like his hero George Lohmann, he was seldom afterwards out of the Cambridge side, winning a Blue for three years. This record was remarkable for two reasons; first, at a time when Varsity Blues came almost entirely from a limited range of famous public schools, Digby Jephson had been educated at a small private school, The Manor House, Clapham. The upper crust world of cricket at Cambridge must have been very strange to him, but in spite of his background he soon made himself acceptable to those of a different social strata, and he certainly enjoyed the atmosphere. The second reason is that with all the excellent cricketers available, Jephson held his place without ever doing anything outstanding. In 43 innings over those three years he scored only 516 runs at an average of 17.2 with a top score of 51, and he took only 7 wickets at a cost of 60 runs each - really a very poor record. But he was a fine fielder, and no one could have shown more enthusiasm. During the last season of 1892, in which he bowled only one over in matches for the University, he unhappily developed a sudden inability to deliver the ball when he reached the bowling crease which seemed to have become a barrier to him; Nick Cook of Northamptonshire has in recent years suffered from the same complaint.

That was the end of Jephson's over-arm bowling, but in the course of much club cricket over the next two years he learnt how to bowl lobs. He recalled that as a boy he had seen Alfred Lyttelton's bizarre lobs in that Test match at the Oval in 1884, he had been well aware of Humphreys' efforts, he had been a victim of J.B. Wood in a Varsity match, and more important, his club cricket had brought him under the influence of the famous W.W. Read, who himself bowled lobs and was a good mentor. Jephson was a ready learner and had enough courage and determination to put up with all the rude remarks and rough treatment that any under-hand bowler must endure.

Jephson soon took many wickets in club cricket with his new delivery, and also scored so freely that in 1894, at a time when Surrey were pursuing a policy of playing plenty of amateurs, the county decided to give him a trial. That year he scored 386 runs at an average of 19.6 with a top score of 94* *v* Essex, but he captured only 6 wickets with his lobs at a cost of 201 runs. It was unfortunate that Surrey's game against the touring South Africans was deemed not first-class, since Jephson had figures of 5 - 18 and 2 - 44 against them, but at least it showed what his lobs could achieve. In the last half of the season Jephson decided to drop county cricket and go on a club tour. This annoyed Surrey so much that he was not invited to play again for the next two years.

It seemed that his first-class career might be over, but in 1897 he returned to the county side, played in 12 matches, and batted extremely well. Though he took only 12 wickets, three of them were against Essex at Leyton when they collapsed from 93 - 3 to 143 all out and lost the match. The *Essex County Chronicle* noted, "As for Jephson's underhands, a little care and patience would soon have enabled the batsmen to deal with him, but they rose to the bait and were 'hooked'." Had Essex won this match they would almost certainly have won the Championship; Jephson did much to rob them, and Surrey were once again Champions.

By 1898 Jephson was well established in the team. The critics who had so harshly attacked him now completely changed their tune; "Mr Jephson has not many superiors among amateurs at the present time", said one. "He is a cricketer from the crown of his head to the soles of his feet," said another. Confidence brought him 38 wickets and he steadily improved on this: 55 wickets in 1899, 66 in 1900 and 77 in 1901, when he also scored 1436 runs. He was appointed captain of Surrey between 1900 and 1902. In 1901 he routed Gloucestershire at the Oval with an analysis of 7 - 51, and he took another 7 wickets off them in the return match, playing his part as opening bowler with Tom Richardson - a dramatic duet.

The feat for which he will ever be remembered was in the match for the Gentlemen v Players at Lord's in 1899. The Gentlemen scored 480 and the Players could score only 196 and 225 in reply. In their first innings the score was taken to 149 before the third wicket fell, but they then folded up against Jephson's lobs.

The Times report reads, "In these days, when a lob bowler's going on is the signal for a laugh from the crowd, it is a great rebuke to those who neglected the development of under-hand slows, that the only good lob bowler we have should get six of England's Players out for 21 runs. Deception in the flight of the ball and ill-timed hitting are the things sought for by a lob bowler, and Mr Jephson certainly had these yesterday and he was backed up by superb fielding. There were many fine catches - and true fielding is a very essential thing for the under-hand bowler - but that by which Mr MacLaren got out Hirst was the catch of the day. It was another hot July day and there were 12,000 present."

Jephson's distinguished victims - all caught - were T. Hayward, W. Brockwell, W. Storer, A.E. Trott, G.H. Hirst and W. Mead. While recognising Jephson's powers of deception, the Press tended to deride the Players: "The failure of the leading professionals of the country against the lobs", said the *Manchester Guardian*, "was truly ludicrous". In the second innings Grace gave Jephson a long bowl of 27 overs, but his lobs were this time played with more respect, and he took only 2 wickets. But for ever this game will be known as "Jephson's Match" - one of the greatest triumphs in lob bowling history.

After resigning the captaincy of Surrey at the end of 1902 Jephson went on playing occasionally until the end of 1904 and he had the satisfaction of obtaining the 'hat-trick' in his last match against Middlesex at the Oval. In a career of 207 matches he had taken 297 wickets at 25 runs each. In *Wisden* he wrote an article entitled *Leg Breaking in 1901* and he finished it with this note on lobsters:

"And now in conclusion, we who stand beneath the tottering pillars, we who bowl the under-hand leg-break - the so-called 'lob' or the so-called 'grub' - 'one ball one nut artists' as they call us in the garbled language of the fair - crave a moment's attention. By himself stands Simpson-Hayward, for he flicks the ball as we have all seen many a wrathful billiard player do when returning the white from the most unexpected pocket - it spins and spins and breaks sharply from the off, and it sometimes hits the wicket. There are two more, Wynyard and myself, and we both bowl in the old, old way, and we bowl with a persistence born of tentative success - occasionally we hook a fish, and great is our rejoicing.

"We are both fond of this bowling, I particularly so, and when on many a ground throughout the country there has arisen on every side the gentle sound of "Take him orf! Take him orf!", were it not that the side comes for ever before oneself, I would bowl and bowl and bowl, until at eventide the cows come home."

In an article in 1903 in the *Country Life* volume on cricket Jephson also wrote: "Lobs act as a stirring tonic to men in the field who have grown lazy and careless from lack of work, for with all the lobs I have ever seen there is always a blissful uncertainty as to where a good batsman will place the next one; and some players hit them so uncomfortably hard that it is best for the slackers to keep their weather eyes open, or they may experience a rude awakening."

We have seen that lobs can employ many different methods of delivery. The Spy cartoon of Jephson published in *Vanity Fair* in 1902 shows him with right hand low, almost bent double, with his back nearly parallel to the ground. His glance is full of deception, he could turn the ball either way and C.B. Fry said that it was his off-break that gained most wickets. He also had a surprise straight ball with hastening top-spin; he had a guileful full pitch (also known as a 'toss') usually aimed on the leg-side and intended to produce a stroke by which the ball ended up in a fielder's hand. Add to this repertoire the 'tice', an enticing steepling high delivery which dropped shorter than imagined. He did not seem to have used the 'donkey drop' falling on the bails, or the 'daisy cutter', now considered 'bad form'. At the turn of the century there was a popular conundrum: "When is a bowler deceitful?" The answer was, "When he is under-hand."

Jephson clearly loved the plotting and planning and careful field placing involved in lob bowling, as well as confounding the critics and their jeers when finally a victim was 'hooked'.

Before dealing with the last of the great lob bowlers - Simpson-Hayward - this seems the moment to note any others of the dwindling party. Jephson mentions Wynyard as his fellow lob-bowler of 'the old, old way'. Major E.G. Wynyard (1861-1936) was an outstanding games player, good enough to have played cricket for England three times, and but for his military duties he would doubtless have played more often. He appeared for Hampshire on and off between 1878 and 1908 and was a real character. Apart from his exciting run-getting he also bowled lobs with zest, taking 66 wickets in his career. His best analysis was 6 - 63. After scoring a brilliant 225 against Lancashire in 1899 he took 5 wickets for 38 runs, and was probably more pleased with his bowling than with his batting. He delivered the ball with his hand held low, like Jephson, and delighted in all the tricks of the trade.

I recently had a letter from the late Geoffrey Cuthbertson who played for three counties in his time, including the captaincy of Northants in the late 1930s. In a keen recollection of Wynyard he tells how as a youngster he was playing at Lord's in an MCC team captained by the famous lob bowler. He writes, "All I can remember is the difficulty I had in returning a catch to Wynyard the bowler from wherever I was fielding. I eventually got the jitters and unfailingly returned the ball half-volley. Teddy (I beg his pardon, Major) Wynyard was rather a fierce old man and I was not popular."

There was a stir of interest when it was announced that there was to be another University lob bowler. G.E. Winter (1876-1923) was educated at Winchester, and won a Blue in 1898-99 chiefly as a result of having figures of 4 - 34 and 6 - 59 against Sussex at Hove, as well as scoring a very rapid 80 runs. In the Varsity match, however, though he opened the bowling, he failed to take a wicket. F.H.E. Cunliffe, of Oxford, wrote: "In 1898 we were rather afraid of him and before the Varsity match we got Humphreys, the old Sussex professional, to give us some practice at the nets." When Sussex met Oxford University at Hove in the same season C.B. Fry was no-balled for throwing by umpire Phillips in his first over and he was "so completely disgusted" that he finished this single over with lobs. In the second innings, at the request of Oxford, C.B. Fry bowled four overs of lobs to give them further practice against such bowling. He also bowled lobs against the Australians at Hove in 1902 when M. A. Noble scored 284.

In 1899 Winter bowled only four overs against Oxford, but he had now been promoted to No. 3 batsman. He played two matches for Middlesex in 1900, and in his whole career took 22 wickets with his lobs at a cost of 23 runs each.

Other contemporary lob bowlers included the following:- A.J. Thornton of Sussex and Kent had a career bag of 27 wickets; W. Wrathall, a leading Gloucestershire bat, also bowled occasional lobs, off one of which Carpenter was caught for 54 at Leyton in 1898; A.J. Turner, of Essex, a fine batsman, was considered to have bowled lobs very poorly, but one very high flighted delivery once got rid of T. Hayward, who is said to have hated lobs; Captain F.W.D. Quinton, of Hampshire, was another good batsman who bowled lobs with one successful analysis of 5 - 93; L.C.H. Palairet, the Somerset man of classic style, had figures of 4 - 133 with lobs when Lancashire made that score of 801 at Taunton in 1895 and MacLaren made his famous 424.

Another outstanding batsman, William Gunn of Notts, took 76 wickets in his career, a number of which were taken by lobs in his later years; in 1893, for example, he had figures of 16 - 1 - 53 - 3 *v* Gloucestershire at Bristol. A report says that, "W.G. Grace hit the first ball of Gunn's lobs very hard indeed to short leg who held it." A typical lob capture. In 1896 F. H Sugg of Lancashire had Ranji easily stumped off one of his lobs to put an end to a match-saving score of 165. E.J. Diver, of Surrey and Warwickshire, who in his time played for both Gentlemen and Players, bowled useful occasional lobs, as did his uncle A.J.D. Diver in the 1850s.

Even Test cricket was to provide a rare example of lob bowling. In the Fourth Test at Melbourne in 1897-8, Australia began badly but with the score at 58-6 Clem Hill and Trumble were to frustrate England with a stand of 165 precious runs. As the runs built up A.E. Stoddart, as captain, decided on desperate measures and went on to bowl lobs. His first over cost 9 runs, and his final spell left him with figures of 6 - 1 - 22 - 0.

When injury and wear and tear caused S.M.J. Woods to cut down on his fiercesome fast bowling, he sometimes took to bowling lobs. He said that he bowled hundreds of them in first-class cricket, but he could not remember having even one victim. However he had numerous catches and stumpings missed off these lobs. On one occasion against the Australians at the Oval he says he might have got the hat-trick, but his dear old friend, Gregor MacGregor, a great wicket-keeper who stood up to the wicket for even his fastest bowling, was flummoxed by the lobs, and missed several chances. Having survived these chances, to quote Woods, "The bounders proceeded to hit me over the pavilion". At another earlier time when playing for Cambridge University Past and Present against the Australians at Portsmouth in 1890, Woods strained his side badly, and was, for perhaps the first time, reduced to bowling lobs. He bowled 10 overs for 41 runs, and several chances were missed off him including an easy stumping by MacGregor which allowed H. Trott to go on to make 186.

MacGregor wrote that Woods said he rather fancied his lobs, but "we never knew if he was in earnest about it." Certainly he never minded being hit - an essential quality in a lob bowler - and he himself said that while his fellow occasional lob bowlers E.G. Wynyard, A.J.L. Hill and Lionel Palairet "all had a little guile about them. Bound to say I hadn't." But for all his apparent lack of success Woods no doubt had a lot of fun with his lob bowling, and was devastating with it in minor cricket.

After the turn of the century there were just a handful more. Sir Arthur Hazlerigg bowled a few lobs for Leicestershire. R.H. Spooner took six first-class wickets with lobs, at a cost of 97 runs each. A.C. MacLaren *v* Worcester in 1910 bowled two overs of 'assorted lobs'. H.S. Altham, playing for Oxford University *v* Hampshire in 1912, bowled a few overs of lobs (4 - 0 - 20 - 0) and had C.B. Fry, who made 203*, missed off him when he had scored 150. After this miss Fry batted facing down the wicket, holding his bat like a croquet-mallet. It is always sad when a lob bowler has chances missed off him since the cause of lob bowling desperately needs the taking of wickets. Altham had bowled lobs at Repton.

Another performer was Major H.B. Bethune. He played twice for Hampshire between 1885 and 1897, and made many large scores in Army and Club cricket. He was also a slow over-arm bowler, but later successfully developed under-arm bowling. In 1901, then aged 56, he played for the Gentlemen of MCC *v* Gentlemen of Holland at the Lansdowne Club, Bath, and completely paralysed the Dutchmen with his under-arm deliveries: he took six wickets for 11 runs in the first innings, and then all ten wickets for 18 runs in the second innings - a remarkable performance against a good team.

Also to be mentioned are C.B. Grace, a son of W.G., who played for London County, and once took 3 - 62 *v* Warwickshire in 1900, these being his only victims. In 1908 P.A. Fryer, on his dèbut for Northamptonshire *v* Leicestershire, had figures of 3 - 36; he was also used as an opening batsman and played in the following match and then no more.

Because he played most of his cricket in Scotland, H.J. Stevenson (1867-1945) had little chance to display his skill more widely; though he played in only 5 first-class matches, he was an exceptionally fine lob bowler. In a reply to E.H.D. Sewell in 1943 about what grip he used, Stevenson explained in detail that there were at least five different grips; one to turn the ball from leg, another to turn the

46

ball from the off, another to create top-spin, a fourth to create under or back spin, and finally the 'dropper' (rather as for top-spin).

He continued with these observations;

"I never had a slip, though I bowled mostly fast ones, the faster the wicket the better, though many who know little of lobs think they want a slow soft wicket. I had point pretty close in and slightly behind the wicket. Extraordinary how many catches Simpson-Hayward got by the striker following the leg-break, pitched on the middle off and going away!

"It's a fascinating play, and if they only knew the fun, and the wonderful number of wickets which lobs get, more of these lads would take the trouble to bowl them. But there are certain conditions, physical and otherwise, wanted in the bowler himself which you don't unfortunately often see combined."

Though George Giffen (1898) says that under-arm bowling remained in vogue in Australia long after it had been discarded in England, there is little evidence over the years of under-hand bowling prospering overseas; perhaps it is difficult to identify the bowler, but there is one fleeting performance that seems quite remarkable. In 1891, in what was the second of the Currie Cup competitions in South Africa, J.H. Piton when bowling for Transvaal *v* Kimberley had two outstanding analyses in Kimberley's totals of 255 and 475. They read (4-ball overs):- 73 - 35 - 82 - 7 and 88 - 36 - 122 - 6.

It was the second first-class match he had played in, but he had not bowled in the first. His whole career covered these two games with Transvaal and three games later with Natal, for whom he bowled only 4 overs for 18 runs. There is a photograph of him bowling, but no information about his style. Those 13 wickets against Kimberley must represent one of the finest match performances ever achieved by a lob bowler.

In this survey of under-arm bowling up to the first War, we have left till the end the last of the truly outstanding lob bowlers, and one with a style that was all his own. It might be imagined that lob bowling can provide little scope for variety of method, but, as we have seen, this is not so. Here now is the strangest of the lot.

After being educated at Malvern, G.H.T. Simpson-Hayward (1875-1936) - then known as G. H. Simpson - went up to Cambridge and played in four matches for the University with fast over-arm deliveries, but he took only one wicket and

47

made few runs. He became tempted to experiment with the bowling of lobs, and this is how it came about:

"I got the idea of bowling lobs from spinning a billiard ball. In my young days I was very fond of playing with small tops which you spin with your fingers in a tray, and this made my fingers very strong, which is a great help in bowling lobs. It struck me that if I could spin an ivory ball, why not a cricket ball, so I set to work, just about the time when I was coming down from Cambridge, to cultivate pitch etc.

"At first I could not pitch the ball at all, so I tried from about 12 yards, and as I improved I retired back until I got the regulation 22 yards. This was done during summer evenings at a net at home bowling to members of the village club, and it took me, on and off, about three years. I learn more every day I bowl, and have to thank Humphreys for some excellent advice. The first time I bowled lobs in a match was at Johannesburg in 1897 when on tour with the Corinthians. I got 8 wickets for 45 runs, I think."

Simpson-Hayward found the fast matting wickets in South Africa much to his liking, as they added extra speed to the ball, which always fizzed off the pitch, especially his off-break which spun fiercely from the flip of his strong fingers.

In 1899 he was invited by Worcestershire to try out his lobs, and he took his first two wickets with them against Hampshire. In 1901 he captured 47 wickets, but for the next five seasons he played very infrequently, taking only 60 wickets over this whole period, though it was in 1903 that he had his best known success. He had been selected to play for the Gentlemen at the Oval, and in the first innings he opened the bowling with W.M. Bradley the Kent fast bowler at the other end. He had no success, but in the second innings with the total at 225 - 6 when the Players needed 295 to win and were going well, W.G. Grace decided to give Simpson-Hayward a spell. This was a good hunch since he finished off the match speedily by taking the last four wickets for 5 runs in 19 balls, to end with an analysis of 7.1 - 0 - 17 - 5; four of the wickets were bowled and the fifth was lbw. It was a real triumph for lob bowling.

In 1908 Simpson-Hayward was able to play more often and took 68 wickets; he took 57 more in the following season, and was then invited to join the England team to tour South Africa in 1909-10. Here, the matting wickets again suited him and he took 23 wickets in the three Test matches, including figures of 6 - 43 and 2

- 59 in the First Test and 5 - 69 in the Third. At first the crowd roared with laughter, but they soon realised how formidable he was. Strudwick, then the England wicket-keeper, tells a good story: "J.W. Zulch, the leading South African batsman, brought a small piece of paper in with him and placed it on the wicket just outside the off-stump. He said, "If Mr Simpson-Hayward pitches outside that piece of paper, I shall play the ball with my legs." Strudwick replied, "I can't have that," and went and picked up the paper. From their very first meeting Zulch, a defensive player, was severely puzzled by Simpson-Hayward, who tended to bowl the first four balls of his spell over the wicket to get his length, and then changed to round the wicket. Zulch, expecting a big off-break, was bowled middle stump by a straight one.

P. F. Warner wrote: "There was no disgrace in falling to Simpson-Hayward, for a cleverer bowler of his kind there never was . . . It was the off-break which spins off the wicket at such a pace which got most of his wickets, but he was far from relying on one type of ball alone. He bowled several different off-breaks, one turning a lot, another six inches, and the third an inch or two."

He did not rely much on flight, but there was his disguised leg-break, the ordinary straight ball, and one that soared high into the air to land on top of the stumps. With one of these donkey-drops he got an lbw decision against that fine Australian hitter, Alan Marshal, after he had scored 176 for Surrey at the Oval in 1908. To quote H. S. Altham, Simpson-Hayward bowled these freakish balls "with effrontery and aplomb."

At the very time when Simpson-Hayward was making such an impact there was a revealing flashback to the days of Clarke when Mr Edward Cutler wrote a letter to *The Times* (24.8.09). He was interested in a recent article on lobs and said, "As one who very often played to Clarke at Eton in the late forties . . . the term 'lobs' is as old to describe a peculiar kind of slow under-hand as 'full-pitch' and 'long-hop' are to denote the sort of ball with which we associate them. We all, even in those days, called W. Clarke 'a pitcher of lobs'. . . . he certainly relied very much on break." The writer of the article on lobs, E.B. Osborn, recalled how when once playing in a village match, he was requested by the captain to "pitch 'em some of your lobs". The good old phrase was still surviving.

H.J. Stevenson, already mentioned as a very talented lob bowler, tells how he sometimes used to bowl in tandem with 'Simmer' about which the bewildered opposition strongly complained. He said that Simpson-Hayward showed him a ball in which "he tucked his thumb into the palm of his hand. The ball lay on the top joint of the thumb and on the flat of the nail. A very telling ball!"

Gilbert Jessop wrote of Simpson-Hayward: "Batsmen found it very hard to know which way the ball was going to turn, an asset that he shared with a googly bowler. His straight ball without break frequently obtained an lbw decision, and it is said that when he bowled this one, he created the noise of the 'flick' associated with his vicious off-break with the fingers of his left hand. This deceived the batsman." Seldom can a cricketer have had stronger power in his fingers. After the South African tour he played less often, and took only 2 wickets in his last two seasons of 1913-4. In the course of his comparatively short career (in number of matches played) he took 503 wickets, and among these victims were most of the best batsmen in England, totally defeated by the sheer nip of his off-break, one of the deadliest balls ever delivered. Here are some of his best analyses: 5 - 38 *v* Warwickshire in 1902; 5 - 11 *v* Leicestershire in 1902; 6 - 78 *v* the Philadelphians in 1903; 6 - 13 *v* Oxford University in 1908; 4 - 19 & 5 - 52 *v* Hampshire in 1908; 3 - 53 & 7 - 54 *v* Middlesex in 1909; 5 - 24 & 3 - 25 *v* Middlesex in 1909; and 5 - 14 *v* Eastern Province in 1909-10. One feature of his bowling was his strike rate of capturing wickets; in the Test series in South Africa he took his 23 wickets at a rate of one every 39 balls. In 1908 his season's bag of 68 wickets had a rate even better.

In the same season J.N. Crawford made the comment; "Lobs are perhaps not always so successful as they might be merely because the performer does not practice them sufficiently." This would not apply to Simpson-Hayward.

This survey up to 1914 of those who have at one time or another bowled under-arm in first-class cricket covers some 75 players, about 30 of whom could be regarded as genuine bowlers, played as part of the team's proper attack. The rest were 'occasionals'. As has been noted, several of them turned to under-arm bowling after previously bowling in a different way. Whatever their motives, they must have our admiration, for to dare to be a lob bowler you must have a spirit of enterprise, invention, great courage and a very thick skin.

Chapter 5

The Post-War Years

It seemed likely that the lost years of the Great War must finally put an end to under-arm bowling in big cricket - dying on a high note with the unique skill of Simpson-Hayward. When county cricket was resumed in 1919 some of the Edwardian glamour of the first-class game had vanished, batting became more sophisticated and bowlers over the last twenty years had been busy exploiting the art of swing and swerve, as well as the leg-break, let alone the mysteries of the googly. There was really little scope for the old-fashioned under-arm bowler. Since then there has been only one under-arm bowler in first-class cricket who has been played purely on his merits as a bowler. He was the last of the line.

Trevor J. Molony (1897-1962) was educated at Repton and played for the XI in 1915. Though he does not appear in the bowling averages in *Wisden*, there is evidence of his taking wickets with his lobs. In 1920 he was at Pembroke College, Cambridge and played in the Freshers match, but did not bowl; later he helped his college to bowl out a strong team of the Incogniti. On a fast and grassy pitch he kept perfect control with his lobs and bowled to a field all but two of whom were on the leg-side. D.L.A. Jephson, then much involved in Cambridge cricket, witnessed Molony's performance with delight; he passed on the information to his old county Surrey, and Molony was included in the annual pre-season trial match at the Oval in April 1921. In the first innings he took Jack Hobbs' wicket - "st Strudwick, b Molony 26" - and, according to Fender, Hobbs gave away his wicket deliberately. In the second innings he took three more wickets, and this persuaded Fender, who was ever-ready to experiment, to select him for the Bank Holiday match against Nottinghamshire at Trent Bridge a few weeks later. Surrey had collapsed for only 76, and Nottinghamshire were going well when Fender put Molony on to bowl. Let *The Cricketer* in its very first issue continue the story:

"The score stood at 170 - 5 when Mr Molony was put on. He is a lob bowler who bowls leg-theory and bowls it accurately, too. He varies the flight of the ball excellently and bowls an exceedingly good full-toss at an awkward height.

"There were four men on the boundary, an outer ring, and four men forming an inner ring, and one man on the off-side at mid-off. The attempts of the last few Nottinghamshire batsmen were ludicrous, and evinced much laughter from the crowd, who showed their unmistakable delight in seeing a lob bowler go on. In any event, bowling as he did wide on the leg-side, very few runs were scored off him, and in desperation several of the batsmen lashed out at his full pitches, with dire results, for they placed them right down the throats of the fieldsmen on the boundary. Payton (19) was taken this way by Mr Reay at fine leg; Barratt (1) was caught at deep square-leg by Shepherd; whilst Whysall (5) attempted to execute an overhead tennis-serve shot through the unguarded covers and succeeded only in plunking the ball into Ducat's hands at mid-off. Richmond was literally halfway up the pitch to one ball, missed it, and scampered back, more or less alongside it, just in time to get into his ground. Both Richmond and Strudwick finished up lying full length on the ground. Rarely has such comic bowling been seen in first-class cricket."

P.G.H. Fender recalls how one wag in the crowd called out: "Don't take him off, Fender. I want to go home and get my old woman. She hasn't had a good laugh for months."

When Notts were all out for 201, Molony ended up with the good figures of 3 wickets for 11 runs from 7 overs, and in the second innings he bowled another 7 overs for only 19 runs, but the batsmen were now more respectful and avoided getting out.

The *Nottingham Journal* made this comment on Molony's bowling: "The lob always was and is a stratagem. Its weakness is its strength because it is unconventional. What would cricket be like if all bowlers adopted the under-hand style? Well, batsmen would learn to score without falling rapidly into simple traps." Molony played again in the next county match against Leicestershire where he had figures of 6 - 1 - 19 - 1 and 7 - 1 - 19 - 0. His only wicket was when he had A. Lord caught by the wicket-keeper Strudwick for 86. This may be the wicket which Fender wrongly attributed to the Nottinghamshire match. He wrote: "Molony bowled so wide of the stumps that one batsman was caught by Strudwick off a full-blooded hit which he had to catch or be almost decapitated. Struddy came up to me afterwards and said: "It's him or me - if you go on playing him I'm off". After that, Molony's days were numbered. But not quite; he was given a third match for Surrey *v* Warwickshire at Birmingham in mid-June, where he bowled only in the second innings for an analysis of 6 - 0 - 21 - 0. That was his last appearance. The Surrey Committee, possibly persuaded by Strudwick's threat, decided not to continue the experiment, nor did Molony play again even in the 2nd XI. However, he went on playing for a long time in club cricket, often with the Repton Pilgrims. We are fortunate to have this account of his bowling by Rex Alston in a letter to *The Cricketer* in 1983:

"I played for Hastings on the Central Ground against Trevor Molony when he was on tour with the Repton Pilgrims, and I faced his fiercesome bowling. I seem to remember that he bowled round the wicket with only one fieldsman on the off-side at extra cover, and the other eight on the leg-side in two rings, an inner from mid-on to backward-leg, and an outer from long-on round to deep fine leg. He ran up quite fast, gave the ball a tweak usually from leg, bowled the occasional grubber, and then let loose a very fast one straight at the batsman's head or chest which was very difficult to put away. There was always the risk that if no shot was played, the ball would drop on the bails. I was consequently highly amused to read of his confrontation with the Nottinghamshire batsmen, three of whom were caught on the leg side swiping at the 'beamer'. . . It would certainly add to the entertainment if a modern 'lobster' played in first class cricket."

So much for Molony whose brief career of three matches in which he took 4 wickets for 89 runs in 33 overs forms a tiny slice of cricket history.

Since then there have been a handful of examples of occasional lobs bowled with the definite intention of getting a wicket when batsmen have seemed specially obdurate. Here are some of the earlier ones:

A.J.L. Hill (1871-1950) was a fine batsman who also varied lob bowling with faster over-arm balls. He was once concerned in an odd incident when bowling lobs for Lord Hawke's XI *v* Griqualand West XV at Kimberley in 1895-6; the batsmen opposing him walked off the field in a huff with complaints of being insulted by being treated with such 'condescension'. Lord Hawke explained that he was not insulting them by using a lob bowler: They ought to have remembered that the South African J.H. Piton had only just previously bowled excellent lobs for

Transvaal. In the Test matches, however, Hill was bowling fastish over-arms and probably bowled this way in obtaining analyses of 7 - 31 *v* Leicestershire in 1897 and 6 - 22 also *v* Leicestershire in 1900. In post-war county cricket, now aged 47, he certainly reverted to lobs against Sussex at Hove in 1919 and had figures of 3 - 11 and 2 - 19. He was well known in club cricket for his serious lob bowling.

Among others at about the same time were C.T.A. Wilkinson who captained Surrey in 1919-20 and bowled some 'last resort' lobs from a low hand against Lancashire at Old Trafford in 1919, when Makepeace was plodding on for 5 1/2 hours, and at Southampton he had figures of 2 - 21 and 3 - 66 with more successful lobs against Hampshire. P.F.C. Williams (1884-1958) bowled very occasional lobs for Gloucestershire with career figures of 2 - 173. James Seymour (1879-1930), a fine Kent batsman, is said to have bowled 3 overs of left-handed lobs when the Australians scored 676 at Canterbury in 1921. H.D. Hake (1894-1975) bowled three overs of lobs *v* Lancashire for Hampshire in 1923. He had bowled lobs in the Public Schools representative match at Lords in 1914, so too had A.D. Denton (1896-1961) who bowled two such overs for Northamptonshire in 1914. A.J. Stevenson, a lob bowler, like his uncle 'H.J.' bowled one over for Scotland *v* Ireland in 1928.

P.R. May (1884-1965) who played as a fast bowler for Cambridge University and Surrey in the early 1900s turned out for the Free Foresters against Cambridge in 1926 and bowled 10 overs of lobs for 52 runs, but took no wicket. When Nottinghamshire met Gloucestershire at Trent Bridge in 1931, their captain, A.W. Carr (1893-1963) had a rare spell of bowling. Gloucestershire had made 117, Nottinghamshire replied with 125, and then Gloucestershire decided to bat out time rather than make any declaration. To save the regular bowlers, and with the game virtually dead, Carr went on and bowled 15 overs for 37 runs and two wickets. In the course of this he bowled "one most subtle lob" to batsman Stephens, who, to quote the *Notts. Guardian*, "was seriousness personified, even when Carr bowled him a lob, his expression of grim determination never altered, although the crowd rocked with laughter." Carr's book *Cricket with the Lid Off* suggested that he bowled a series of lobs and took wickets with them, but this was not so.

When once asked for a comment during the 'Bodyline' trouble in Australia in 1932/33, A.W. Carr replied: "All I can suggest regarding the controversy is that Jardine should make Larwood bowl under-hand."

At that moment many of the Nottinghamshire bowlers were suffering an injury and Carr evidently enjoyed this chance to bowl. In the next match he went on as an over-arm opening bowler, and to his great delight he clean bowled Herbert Sutcliffe for 4, and in the next game he again bowled. On the first day of the match *v* Warwickshire at Birmingham he bowled his usual over-arms when they scored 394 - 3, and when they continued to bat next day he tried five overs of lobs for the cost of 31 runs, but without success.

When Nottinghamshire had a centenary day in 1938 the chairman is said to have stated that he was sure lob bowling could still be successful and that in fact four members of the team were religiously practising lobs, but this claim was probably a bit of a joke by Kenneth Rankin, *The Daily Telegraph* reporter.

Grahame Parker told me how during his enterprising period of captaincy of Gloucestershire in the 1930s, B.H. Lyon was sometimes ready to consider the possibility of under-hand bowling. On one opening day some Midland county were snailing away before lunch at Bristol. Lyon had already given the opposing batsmen some 'advice' and then threatened to bowl the last over himself. "I'll bowl an over of grubbers or perhaps it will be an E.M. one," which meant an over of howitzer balls with which E.M. Grace once created havoc at the Oval. As for the grubber it was intended to be a ball that just reached the block, as though aiming at the jack in Bowls. He announced his intention to the whole field, and the look on the batsman's face showed that he had made his point. This was not the only time Lyon made such a protest, but we have no evidence of his actually delivering an over of under-arms.

A much more important example of under-arm bowling was the experiment by J.C. Clay (1898-1973) who was a top-class bowler who took well over 1000 wickets for Glamorgan. Originally a fast bowler, he later changed to off-spin, and won an England cap in 1935.

When Glamorgan played Leicestershire at Cardiff in 1933 the visitors scored 365 - 4 on a very hot opening day and Alan Shipman was batting in his most stubborn mood. At 6 o'clock, Clay, always enterprising, decided to bowl some lobs to him, and to the delight of the crowd, having scored 145 Shipman was clean bowled by one of these. He was full of smiles as he walked out and said that the ball turned quite a foot. An eye-witness wrote, "I shall never forget it. Clay was so jubilant that he did a kind of highland fling, and the rest of the team flopped on the ground laughing convulsively." Next day Leicester went on batting until they declared at 461 - 6. Clay again bowled lobs - 4 overs for only 7 runs. One ball he simply rolled down the wicket *a la* bowls to Armstrong, who just blocked it. He also bowled several full tosses to leg, but Armstrong remained unmoved.

Later in the season, against Somerset at Weston, Clay again bowled some lobs and had Wellard caught and bowled for 65. He may well have bowled lobs at other times, since he believed that a good lob bowler could take masses of wickets. Had he decided to bowl lobs more often, no one could have made a better job of it.

There are also a few odd references to the occasional lob; in 1922-3 A.E. Liddicut is said to have bowled a lob when M.CC were scoring 282 - 0 to save the game against Victoria at Melbourne, and this ball was a wide. I.B. Cromb of New Zealand started to bowl lobs in the Fourth Test match at Christchurch in 1935-6 when England were struggling successfully to save the game. In the same season the massive Maharajah of Patiala took two wickets with lobs when playing for a visiting Australian team against Patiala. R.J.O. Meyer, probably at Bath in 1947, when he was captaining Somerset, bowled the occasional high tossed lob.

J. B. Iverson, the Australian bowler with an odd finger grip, when on tour in India with a Commonwealth XI in 1953-4, bowled a lob and took a wicket with it.

There might well have been one other very interesting newcomer to the list of lob bowlers. At a time when he was the fastest bowler in England, Arthur Gilligan was hit over the heart by a ball in the Gentlemen *v* Players match at Lord's in 1924. After being told that he would never bowl fast again, he defied the doctors and tried to bowl as before; after a few overs, however, he realised that fast bowling was over for him. He writes, "I thought of becoming a lob bowler, and getting a hundred wickets a year in this way, but a bowler, unless he is a genius cannot change his mode of bowling all of a sudden like this." Luckily he was to recover enough to bowl at reduced pace, so his idea of lob bowling came to nothing.

There may be several reasons for the bowling of the occasional lob; it may be bowled out of a sheer irritation; purely for fun; as the only way of finishing an over after being injured or continually no-balled; out of kindness to the batsman; as a protest at a declaration being delayed. Some examples of each reason follow:

Irritation. One day, probably at Portsmouth in 1928, the maverick George Brown of Hampshire became so annoyed at the stone-walling tactics of the

Somerset batsman, C. C. Case, that he measured out a 40 yard run, galloped up, and then rolled down a slow under-arm all along the ground. Case, taken by surprise, missed the ball and it bowled him, but the umpire rightly said 'Not Out!' since Brown had not announced his intention of changing his mode of delivery; those intending to bowl a lob are inclined to forget about this Law.

Just for fun. At Glastonbury in 1964 Somerset needed only 3 runs to beat Sussex with 8 wickets in hand. Ken Suttle was bowling and the third of his "along the ground" balls was hit for 4 and victory. He said typically that he was bowling these lobs 'purely for fun'.

No-balled for throwing. In 1942 when playing for Trinidad against Barbados Mobarak Ali had problems with his off-breaks when he was no-balled 30 times for throwing. In the end he was reduced to finishing the over with slow under-arm grubs. The unfortunate G.M. Griffin of South Africa when playing in an exhibition game at Lord's in 1960 after the Test match had ended early, was once again no-balled for throwing, and on the advice of his captain turned to under-arm deliveries. The first of these was again no-balled as he had given no warning of this change of delivery, but he at last ended what was an 11 ball over with a series of legal lobs. That was the end of his career as a bowler.

A more valid reason for having to finish an over with lobs was when an injury prevented the normal over-arm delivery, though it is now legal for another bowler to be called upon to finish the over. Before this sensible change, however, C.F. Root, for Derbyshire *v* Somerset at Taunton probably in 1913, broke down after the first ball of one over, straining his back in a deep foothole. (Such footholes can now be filled in). Root writes, "I was compelled to finish the over by means of lobs, and A.E. Newton dispatched three of the five remaining balls to the boundary."

Kindness. When MCC met Victoria at Melbourne in 1929-30 the home side went in on the fourth day with only 7 runs to win. This was soon reduced to 3 runs, so with rain falling F. Barratt, usually a fast bowler, sent down a slow under-arm delivery to Woodfull, whose score was 96*. Woodfull drove it towards the boundary, but it suddenly stopped just short of the fence. When the batsmen saw this they quickly came back to run four and Woodfull got his hundred, though properly his innings should have been 99*, as the match was won on the third run.

Another form of 'kindness' was when a batsman was helped on his way towards some target such as a century by offering him friendly bowling. In the

Roses match at Old Trafford in 1899 Yorkshire made 344 to which Lancashire replied with 450. In Yorkshire's second innings on the third evening with only a few minutes left David Denton had scored 89*: MacLaren then put himself on to bowl an over of what was described as some sort of lobs; Denton hit three fours off these balls bowled on the leg side, and reached his century. The stumps were then pulled up. The *Manchester Guardian* said that this may have been a kindly act on MacLaren's part, but that "it was not cricket".

As a protest. It is sad to find that a fair proportion of examples of occasional lob bowling since 1919 have been produced as some kind of protest against the opposition, usually when they have seemed too reluctant to make a declaration. Such deliveries totally devalue the good name of lob bowling, but may have been effective in rousing the spectators to show their feelings. There seem to have been few examples of such protest bowling in pre-War days, but when Lancashire played Sussex at Hove in 1905 they carried on batting into the second day until lunchtime when their score was 587 - 8. Though allowed now to declare, they continued after lunch and C.B. Fry in disgust ordered C.L.A. Smith and H.P. Chaplin to bowl daisy-cutters, and soon the Lancashire captain, A.C. MacLaren, did declare at 601 - 8.

P.G.H. Fender, who had bowled lobs in school matches at St Paul's in 1909 and had a grandfather who was expert at such bowling, might well have tried his hand at lobs at any time, but the only definite evidence of his bowling them was against Hampshire at Bournemouth in 1931. He considered that the Hampshire captain, Giles Baring, with a lead of 330 should not have batted on after lunch. He also showed his displeasure by making every fielder change over completely when a left and right handed batsman were in together at the same time; Fender ticked off Sandham for hurrying, and one over took 12 minutes. The crowd who had barracked Baring for not declaring sooner, now also booed Fender for his slowing-down tactics.

In their match against Yorkshire at the Oval in August 1933 Surrey batted all the first day and then went on until after lunch on the second day before M.J.C. Allom declared at 560 - 6, the highest score reached against Yorkshire for 32 years. When Surrey surprisingly continued after lunch Hedley Verity, bowling from the Pavilion end, protested to Tom Barling, the batsman, and in some disgust said, "If you want to make a farce of this, I'll bowl you some lobs next over!" He packed the leg-side with fielders scattered anywhere, and began the over with a lob, for which he was duly no-balled by Chester, the umpire. Verity enquired why, and Chester explained that he had not announced his change of delivery. He then bowled another lob - also no-balled - and Barling hit it for six. The score-book shows that this over included one no-ball, not scored off, and another one hit for six.

In the last stages of the match Yorkshire, after being out for 233, followed on and scored 219 - 5 to save the game, but to prevent Surrey from taking the new ball, refused to make runs. R.J. Gregory, a slow bowler, ended with figures of 12 - 11 - 1 - 0. It was not a very edifying game.

When Nottinghamshire met Glamorgan at Trent Bridge in 1951 the visitors batted very slowly on the first day - at one time only 12 runs from 15 overs on a perfect pitch - and by tea time with only 220 runs scored, the Nottinghamshire captain Reg Simpson became annoyed. Let his opposing captain, Wilf Wooller, tell the story: "We batted very slowly and suddenly Reg lost his nut. He put himself on at the pavilion end and announced: "I'm going to bowl under-hand." As sometimes happens with rubbish bowling we almost made a mess of it. I nearly got out, and Willy Jones was so upset that he lost his wicket. Reg Simpson and I were great pals and we laughed about it afterwards." Though Simpson bowled only one over of lobs, he conceded only 2 runs to Wooller who played him with utmost caution and was once hit on the pads. But the over had some effect as Glamorgan shortly were to lose 4 wickets for 11 runs.

Sussex scored 379 - 9 dec. against Glamorgan at Hove in 1956 and then dismissed Glamorgan for 64. Following on, they were determined to save the game and ended up at 200 - 1, of which Wooller scored 79* in 6 1/2 hours. R.G. Marlar was so frustrated that he bowled a few lobs to Wooller, but without any success.

In the following season the two teams met again at Hastings. Batting first Sussex, in order to repay Glamorgan for their efforts of 1956, deliberately batted extremely slowly. On the second day Wooller bowled the last five balls of the day as under-arms to Marlar who swung at every one without making contact. Marlar later dismissed the incident as a bit of fun, but it is not surprising that Wooller should be concerned in all these last three incidents of protest bowling. He could at times be provocative, but could also enjoy the joke afterwards.

When Leicestershire were playing Sussex at Leicester in 1977, Ray Illingworth considered that the Sussex captain, Peter Graves, was postponing the declaration too long, and bowled a full over of lobs in protest. While he was bowling this over the strains of Elgar's Pomp and Circumstance were coming full blast from a neighbouring pub.

In 1978 when Sussex met Surrey at Hove, they had scored 301 - 4 dec, and Surrey had reached 321, and time was going on. As a reminder to the Surrey captain, that a declaration was due, Mike Buss bowled 4 under-arm balls along the ground. Surrey did declare at 328 - 7, and the game ended in an exciting finish, so perhaps this protest had done some good.

According to Graeme Fowler in his book *Fox on the Run*, when England played against West Zone during the 1984-5 tour of India, they batted well into the second day, which annoyed the home side. He wrote, "the England batsmen messed around with Vengsarkar bringing himself on to bowl lobs." D.B. Vengsarkar, captain of West Zone, bowled only one over (1 - 0 - 7 - 0), but later enhanced his protest by batting 8 hours for a score of 200*.

Oxford University when playing Lancashire at Oxford in 1990 were so irritated at the county's reluctance to declare that P. Gerrans, an Australian, bowled an under-arm ball. As he gave no warning of his change of delivery he was promptly no-balled.

So much for these 'protest' incidents which are a travesty of serious underarm bowling. Here now are a few more bits and pieces. There might well have been another name on the list of lob bowlers - that of C.T. Bennett, the Harrovian who played for Cambridge in 1923 and 1925. D.L.A. Jephson, who was closely concerned with University cricket, had high hopes that Bennett might train on to produce lobs in first-class cricket, but his hopes came to nothing. C.H.B. Pridham in an article in *The Cricketer* in 1948 wrote of a certain Captain J.R.S. Mackay who during 1921 took 225 wickets with lobs mostly in the West Indies, and he also wrote that at about the same time in Egypt a nameless left handed lob bowler took countless wickets by turning the ball almost at right angles on the matting wicket. He was last heard of serving a term of imprisonment.

There must be others later who bowled lobs in good club cricket; but it is difficult to trace them. Of one there is good evidence; the father of Eric Hollies, the Warwickshire and England spin bowler, for many years used to bowl lobs for Old Hill in the Birmingham League. In 1929 father and son (then aged just 17) dismissed Moseley between them. In the previous season Bill Hollies had taken

A fine sketch of G.H.Simpson-Hayward by James Thorpe

Left: G.H.Simpson-Hayward

Below: Simpson-Hayward's grips for the leg-break

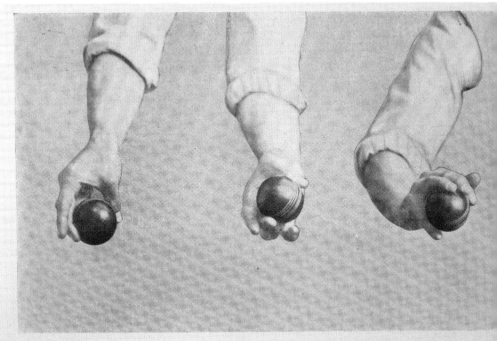

G. H. SIMPSON-HAYWARD

1. Leg-break
(Act of delivery, does not turn so much as No. 2)

2. Leg-break

3. Leg-break
(Act of leaving hand)

Walter Humphreys of Sussex and England

OFF • **LEG**

Above: Trevor Molony of Surrey - last of the line?

Left: Field for Molony's bowling

100 wickets and was known as "the Twiddle-dee-dee King". C.H. Palmer, then aged only 14, has recollection of playing with Bill Hollies in 1933 and his career went on for several more years. He is said to have learnt his under-arm skill by practising bowling at the wicket with a barrel placed in front of it. He must be one of the few lob bowlers to appear in good league cricket at such a late date.

Lobs have been so rare in recent times that it seems reasonable to mention more examples other than in first-class cricket. In 1933 Cdr. R.J. Shaw R.N. bowled an over of lobs in a 2-day match against the RAF at Lord's. Bill Andrews when captaining Somerset 2nd XI v Cornwall in 1950 was so annoyed at the Cornish captain's delay in declaring that he started bowling lobs and had a batsman caught deep on the leg-side off one of them.

A more recent example came in the Minor Counties Challenge match of 1974. Oxfordshire were challenged by Cornwall and were so determined not to lose that in their second innings they batted for nearly four hours to score 194 - 6 before declaring. Cornwall left only 70 minutes to score 288. D.J. Halfyard of Cornwall was so frustrated that in one over he sent down an under-arm delivery and three donkey-drops. The next bowler, B. Laity, a right arm bowler, took to bowling some balls with his left arm.

I have mentioned that sometimes a bowler produces a lob without notifying the umpire and batsman of change of delivery, and thereby gets no-balled for it. On one rare occasion the bowler - none other than the great S. F. Barnes - defeated the umpire who forgot to call no-ball. Glamorgan were playing Staffordshire in 1912, and Creber, the last man in for Glamorgan, for some reason decided to bat right-handed to Bucknell, and then change to left-handed when facing Barnes. Barnes surprisingly entered into the spirit of this farcical move, and turned the tables on Creber by skittling the ball down under-hand without warning, amidst a roar of laughter. Creber missed the ball and was promptly given out lbw when the umpire should have called no-ball. The Glamorgan captain protested to the umpire about this, but the lbw decision had to stand in what was Barnes' most unusual victim of his career.

Lobs seem rare overseas, but there is said to have been a lob bowler in Grade C cricket in Sydney in the 1930s, and A.L. Mann, who played for Australia v India in 1977-78, had a father who used to bowl fast under-hand spinners. Recently John M. Dew wrote to me from Mont Albert, Victoria to say that in 1947/48 he played in a Grade B match at Melbourne and faced an under-arm bowler. He writes, "At first my batting partner could not believe it when 'under-arm' was announced. . . . the look of Alan remains with me. He asked again and got the same reply. Then began laughing. The bowler ran in from about 10 paces and whipped them down left-handed on a good length, and nearly bowled Alan. I guess the element of surprise got him some wickets." The bowler's name was Robert Barbour, and he bowled lobs only occasionally. He normally bowled slow over-arm.

There was still the odd grub, the ball bowled all along the ground with the deliberate intention of preventing the batsman scoring at a critical moment. Lord Harris (1851-1932), that great stickler for the decencies of cricket, was originally a fast round-arm bowler, but in his later years he took to lobs, and had at least one first-class wicket when he had P. Shivram of the All India XI caught in a match v Kent at Catford in 1911. Harris continued to play cricket to a great age, and in 1922, then aged 71, was playing for the Lords and Commons against a team from Canada. The visitors were replying to a score of 136 - 9 d; the ground was wet but they were making good progress when Harris went on to bowl fast under-hand sneaks to keep the runs down. Lord Gorell, who was playing in that match wrote: "From the wet ground, the divots flew as well as words, square leg was besmattered with mud, and there was some booing among the spectators, but Harris took 2 - 20 in 8 overs with a leg-side field, and the Canadians were struggling at 123 - 6 at the close."

This was not the first time that a visiting team from America was treated in a way that might have been considered shabby. A side from Merion, Philadelphia were playing a Kent Club and Ground side at Tonbridge in August 1914. They needed to score 153 runs in 55 minutes to win the game, and the magazine *The World of Cricket* reported that when only 2 more runs were wanted "the last two balls of the game were rolled along to the ground to prevent their being hit - rather an inglorious device." The instruction (probably to R.T. Bryan) to bowl these two grubs must have come from G.J.V. Weigall, the Kent captain; the team also included Fairservice, as well as J.L. Bryan (then aged 18), R.T. Bryan (16) and W.H. Ashdown, who at the age of 15 had already appeared in a first-class match. It seems odd to us now that two such devoted cricketers as Lord Harris and Weigall should have indulged in such doubtful (though quite legal) tactics against visiting teams who had come to England to learn all the niceties and proprieties of the game. In quite recent times a similar incident was to shake the cricket world and caused hands to be raised in horror.

On February 1st, 1981 in the penultimate match of the unending Benson and Hedges World Series of one-day games, New Zealand were facing a score of 235 by Australia and when the last over of the game began they still needed 15 runs to win with 4 wickets left. Hadlee hit a 4 off the first ball and was out off the second, Smith then hit 2 twos, and was bowled off the fifth ball; so 6 runs were wanted off the last delivery. Greg Chappell, the captain, told the bowler, his brother Trevor, to bowl this last ball to Brian McKechnie as an under-arm sneak from which he could not possibly hit a six. He informed the umpire Don Wiser of his intention to change his delivery, he bowled the ball along the ground, no six was hit, and so Australia won the match.

This action led to a furore of complaint from all quarters. The Australian Cricket Board 'met' by telephone to condemn the deed and suggested that in this competition underarm bowling should be banned forthwith. The chairman of the New Zealand Cricket Council described Chappell's action as "the worst sporting action" he had ever seen. Sir Donald Bradman "totally disapproved". Richie Benaud referred to "a disgraceful happening". It was even suggested that Australia's ambassador to New Zealand should be recalled as a protest. Greg's brother Ian in his forthright way wrote: "Fair dinkum Greg, how much pride do you sacrifice to win 35,000 dollars?", and the sporting Keith Miller stated "yesterday one-day cricket died and Greg Chappell should be buried with it."

Under this barrage of criticism Chappell not unnaturally said it was something he would not do again and realised that what he had done was morally wrong. He said that he had ordered the action on the spur of the moment; he must have done some quick thinking. Dennis Lillee, who was playing said he felt at the time that there would be an uproar, but it was all quite legal, and if Greg had asked him to bowl under-arm he would have done so for the sake of the side.

The day after the affair Doug Walters promised to show Allan Border on the Sydney ground just how that grub might have been successfully dealt with. He asked Border to bowl a grub to him and the moment the ball was delivered Walters charged down the wicket and stuck out his left foot whereupon the grub cannoned into his boot, popped up in the air, and then Walters clouted it out of the ground. He was too far down the wicket for there to be any risk of lbw. What a pity the New Zealand batsman did not think of this at the time; it might seem to have made a glorious story of the victory of good over evil. Unfortunately, however, Walters forgot (as would many others) that the Law for being out for Hitting the

Ball Twice is not concerned only with hitting the ball twice with the bat. Law 34 reads: "The striker shall be out on appeal if, after the ball is struck or stopped by any part of his person, he wilfully strikes it again with his bat or person, except for the whole purpose of guarding his wicket."

By pushing out his foot to make the ball jump up and then hitting it with his bat, Walters is causing a clear infringement of the Law, and if McKechnie had in fact done what Walters so ingeniously suggested, he should have been given out for doing so.

So Greg Chappell by his action made sure that Australia won the match, and it comes to mind that Lord Harris and G.J.V. Weigall who had indulged in a similar act would surely have commended Chappell for his clever ploy; fifteen years later, however, Chappell again repudiated it and claimed that it was due to some mental lapse. He could never have imagined the outcry that was to result from it, even to the extent of producing a special amendment to one of the Laws.

With the most helpful assistance of Test Match umpire Don Oslear it has been possible to trace the subsequent results of Trevor Chappell's single notorious delivery. Don Oslear was in New Zealand at the time and tells me that when returning by car from a match in which he had been umpiring he listened on the radio to the last moments of that Benson & hedges match in which the home country had been deliberately thwarted of any possible chance of winning. He writes; "As the players left the field with the batsman unhappy, and the fielders not appearing to show delight, the crowd rose as one man and the booing did not cease until some minutes after the players had left the field. I have never heard a sound like it. . . and I never wish to hear it again."

As a result of the protests a decree was brought in by the TCCB under the 'Special Regulations' which are associated with the Laws; under-arm bowling was for the 1982 season outlawed by the TCCB for all their competitions and that included First-Class matches (except Test Matches) and One-Day Prudential Trophy matches. The regulation also applied for the 1983 season, but at the end of that summer and before the beginning of the next one, the legislators wisely felt that since 'under-arm bowling' was part of the history of the game, it should be allowed. This was when the present regulation was written as set down below;

64

"LAW 24 (1)   No ball, mode of delivery

All Matches

LAW 24 (1) will apply, but in addition the umpire at the bowler's end shall call and signal 'No Ball' if a ball which the umpire considers to have been delivered,

(i)   Bounces more than twice, or

(ii)   Rolls along the ground, or

(iii)   Comes to rest before it reaches the striker or if not otherwise played by the striker before it reaches the popping crease."

There has been some unfortunate misunderstanding about the present legality of under-arm bowling. The special regulations just quoted concerned only cricket conducted by the TCCB (cricket bodies overseas may also have their own special regulations). All other forms of cricket are covered by cricket LAW which has no restriction at all on a ball being delivered under-arm in any manner.

The one really sad feature of the Chappell story is that his action gave all under-arm bowling a bad name, and helped merely to discourage those who were tempted to bowl under-arm. Since then anyone, anywhere, attempting to bowl lobs would be liable to be accused of behaving unfairly, every ball would be regarded as an unsporting sneak, and even the very delivery in itself improper. In a club game of fairly recent time the captain of a side, one of whose bowlers was taking wickets with excellent lobs, once felt honour bound to apologise to the victims. Can there be any thinking more muddled than that?

The under-arm story need not end, however, on an unhappy note. One of the finest of cricketing brains, that of Michael Brearley (b 1942) conceived the idea that under-arm bowling could even in these days have its value, and he made a brave and determined effort to put this idea into practice. He has written, "This was not, I should stress, to be bowled as a protest, but as a practised last resort." He first bore this out in his Cambridge days in at least two matches: "I didn't enter into the idea hastily. I had an under-arm stumping chance against Sussex. The batsman came down the wicket, missed the ball, and the wicket-keeper missed the stumping chance. That was a pity, it would have shut everybody up."

In the last moments of a drawn Varsity match later in that season of 1963, Brearley, the captain, bowled two overs of lobs and not a run was scored off him.

Several years later when he was captaining Middlesex he again attempted lob bowling: "In 1980 for Middlesex I bowled a few lobs myself when we were stuck or trying to winkle someone out. On the whole they were not approved of by our team, let alone the opposition (I was terrified that Brian Davison was going to split my head open with his bat after the first lob I bowled to him.) Nor were they successful. My season's bowling figures were: 15.4 overs, 65 runs, no wickets." Among these lobs were what Phil Edmonds called 'moonballs', extremely high overarm full-tosses designed to land on top of the bails. Edmonds commented that it was possible to embarrass a batsman out: "not to hit a really bad bowler looks like incompetence, but getting out to such a bowler looks even worse."

Brearley considered that it was not impossible for the art of lob bowling to be revived to some extent, and that it was "a good freakish variation if you are stuck", but there were great difficulties for the man who attempted it. In a letter to me he wrote: "I was a bit intimidated by the conservative and critical attitudes of others in and around the game. That's why I didn't develop the skills of underarm or lob bowling. It seemed not worth riding the opposition which was often intense".

This was a great shame because if one man could have achieved even the glimmer of a revival it was Mike Brearley. He possessed all the enterprise and courageous qualities needed for such bowling. It was a fine effort that deserved more success.

So ended - for the time being - the story of under-arm bowling in first-class cricket over the last post-1918 years. Some 25 names have been mentioned with a wide range of motives, but only a handful have been serious performers. But even the occasional protest lob has brought a stir amongst the spectators, and even a laugh or two. It reminds them that first-class cricket can still possess an element of entertainment - a feature that often now seems to have been forgotten. Perhaps, perhaps there may one day be another to follow in Brearley's enterprising footsteps.

There are also one or two dramatic 'might-have-beens'. In the mid-1960s there might have been a most spectacular display of under-arm bowling. Between 1961 and 1966 the captain of Glamorgan was Ossie Wheatley, and he once invited a local Cardiff baseball pitcher to come to the nets for half an hour to show what he could do as an under-arm bowler with a perfectly legal delivery. Paddy Hennessy approached the crease from about 15 yards and whipped in yorkers and toe crushers at a speed that matched a genuine fast-medium bowler; so effective was he that Glamorgan considered playing him in the next county match, but second thoughts prevailed, and to quote Tony Lewis, "we lost courage". In a letter to me he went on to discuss the possibility of Hennessy playing in county cricket and wrote: "How near did he come to being selected? It was so improbable that the answer is, I guess, a long way from selection for a County Championship match, but we were a side of spirit in those days and it was not too unlikely that we would take a chance. Ossie Wheatley was the captain and Peter Walker the main urger. Hennessy bowled extremely fast yorkers and of course the extremely tall Walker was the one who got into most trouble when facing him in the nets. It certainly sharpened us up!"

What a remarkable and fresh experience it would have been for all if Glamorgan had resolved to take the chance; George Brown of Brighton in the 1820s would have lived again, and sleeping dogs on the boundary would have had a rude awakening. There could have been yet another exciting use of lobs quite recently. I was listening to the frustrating last hour's play in the Third Test *v* Australia at Sydney in January 1995. With victory in sight England were restricted to the use of their slow bowlers when trying to capture the last few wickets. Because of the poor light, the introduction of fast bowlers would have meant the end of play.

As the minutes ticked by Geoffrey Boycott when commentating suddenly said that what was needed was something different; "Why not bowl a few under-hand lobs or even something in the Spedegue manner? (to which one of his colleagues asked who did he play for.) Boycott was right; it was just the moment for some daring surprise or experiment, anything to upset the batsmen's rhythm in their successful defensive tactics. A few lobs from Tufnell might just have done the trick.

Chapter 6

Club Cricket and Schools

This survey of under-arm bowling has been largely centred on first-class cricket, but remember that such bowling had a much more extensive life in club and school cricket. The difficulty is to find the evidence; even that concerning schools must be taken from those who are lucky enough to have been playing at Lord's, and from occasional snippets of reminiscence. We hear for example from Lord Harris that in the Eton *v* Harrow match at Lord's in 1860 R.H.L. Burton and R.D. Walker bowled fast sneaks for Eton and between them took 10 wickets. Another of the Walker brotherhood, 'I.D.' took 9 Eton wickets with fast under-hands in the match of 1862. In 1882 E.H. Buckland when playing for Marlborough *v* Rugby clean bowled the first four batsmen with fast grubs. He later played for Oxford and Middlesex.

Lob bowling in the schools seems to have been flourishing in the 1880s, and in the Badminton Library volume on *Cricket* (1888) A.G. Steel wrote, "Every school should possess a lob bowler; if he be a good one so much the better, but one of some sort there must be. Lobs have always been destructive to boys, and even very indifferent lobs are occasionally fatal to schools. A little practice will teach any boy to bowl them fairly; he must bowl round the wicket, must take a long and rather a quick run 'to get fire on the ball' and bowl just fast enough to prevent the batsman hitting the good length balls before they pitch."

Here is a good example of their unexpected success. In 1900 when Leeds Grammar School met Pocklington School, they faced a total of 100 and the opening pair had reached 47 and seemed to be cruising to victory. At this point Miles I'Anson was brought on in desperation to bowl lobs: usually a fast bowler, he had recently injured his arm, and to amuse himself he had been practising lobs but only in the nets. He now put these lobs into serious action, and it was not long before he had taken all ten of the Leeds School wickets, they were all out for 68, and the match was unexpectedly won. The perfect fairy story of what lobs can do.

A similar success in school cricket was recorded in 1921. When Shaftesbury Grammar School 2nd XI met Milton Abbey School, Blandford, G.F. Simpson, bowling lobs for Shaftesbury, took all ten wickets in an innings for 23 runs.

Another school story is worth telling. In their book *Cricketers in the Making* (1950) Trevor Bailey and Denys Wilcox wrote, "A match was played between two famous public schools. Each school had a good XI, one future England bowler and two future University and county cricketers were taking part in the match. At a critical moment in the game a lob bowler came on. It was probably the first time that the batsmen had played under-hand bowling since they were six or seven. The bowler, incidentally a future Davis Cup tennis player, would bowl one ball high, another at medium height and another he would send low and fastish. He bowled intelligently and accurately, moreover he set an attacking field with a silly mid-off a few yards from the bat. It was pitiful to see promising schoolboy batsmen trying to cope with it. They would either try to hit every ball out of the ground or treat it with a respect which was as ridiculous as it was agonising to watch. Three wickets fell almost at once, one well caught at silly mid-off. Lob bowling won the match in good-class public school cricket. It was a tragedy for the batting side, but nevertheless an illuminating experience for all present."

I enquired of Trevor Bailey more details of this match, but he regretted that this story had been written by Denys Wilcox, who alas died at an early age, so it will not be easy to identify it. It might have been a match in 1925 in which Repton were concerned because that team contained H.W. Austin (Davis Cup player) as well as B.H. Valentine and R.H.C. Human, who were to become county players.

It has been possible to identify a few incidents of lob bowling in school cricket of the past. Though there was nothing to equal the record of 1914 when H.D. Hake and A.D. Denton both bowled lobs in the big representative school games, in the Rugby v Marlborough match at Lord's in 1922 the Marlburian C.R.W. Ashfield turned the game round by taking three vital wickets with his lobs and took two more wickets in the second innings. So Rugby lost in spite of having had much practice during the term from a good lob bowler, M.C. Bradby, of the famous Rugby family. In the Eton v Harrow match of 1931, E.B. Peel, of Harrow, bowled three overs of lobs from the pavilion end, but took no wicket. In 1933 D.A.S. Day, son of A.P. Day, topped the Tonbridge bowling averages with 13 wickets for 167 runs, and bowled his lobs in the Clifton match at Lord's. Next year, again at Lord's, he had a wonderful game *v* Clifton for apart from scoring 71 and 130* he also had analyses of 2 - 34 and 2 - 18; he later bowled 5 overs of lobs for the Lord's schools against The Rest. In 1938 R.M. Chaplin played for Harrow *v* Eton at Lord's. He had been bowling lobs during the season, including an analysis of 4 - 30 against Harrow Wanderers.

The last time that a lob bowler was chosen for a big representative school match purely as a bowler was when H.W. Leatham played for the Public Schools *v* MCC at Lord's in 1910. He had earned his place by taking 41 wickets for Charterhouse at a cost of under 10 runs each. He later played in one first-class match in 1914, and took a wicket.

These are just a few random examples of lobs being bowled in school matches at Lord's. We shall never know how frequently they have been bowled elsewhere.

If schoolboys became increasingly reluctant to bowl lobs some of their elders had no hesitation, often with great success. Philip Trevor in his book *Problems of Cricket* (1907) devoted a whole section to lob bowling and told how when he was captaining a side against a public school, "The boys were making runs readily so I went on to bowl lobs from the end which had the low setting sun at my back. Some of the team thought that this was a 'low' trick, but one boy who was scoring freely deliberately kept hitting the ball high in the air knowing that no fielder could see the ball against the sun. It seems that batsmen were allowed to use the low sun tactically, but not the bowlers." An interesting story.

Lord Harris when playing at a fair old age for P.F. Warner's XI *v* Westminster School in 1917 aggressively used every trick of his lobs to get the batsmen out, giving no quarter. Even as late as 1957 we hear of R.J.O. Meyer helping to defeat Wellington School, Somerset by the use of tempting high tossed lobs. The school captain was so upset by this that he wrote a letter to *The Times* suggesting that Meyer's bowling smacked of 'gamesmanship' not proper to use against boys. Could the time come when county cricketers will regard leg-spinners as 'unfair' as being an outmoded form of delivery? My four-year old grandson has already banned me from bowling what he calls 'twiddlers'.

If under-arm bowling is agreed to be highly effective against schoolboy batsmen, why then have not the schools given more encouragement to them?

Writing in 1946 that most forthright of cricket writers E.H.D. Sewell thought he knew the answer: "It is because games masters and coaches are, in many cases, funks. Boys themselves funk trying to bowl the stuff because they think it looks foolish to do so." One of the most recent examples of under-arm bowling in school cricket was that of Stewart Furber who bowled in this way for Bristol Grammar School 2nd eleven in about 1965.

There is no doubt that an intelligent and strong-minded boy, if properly encouraged by his mentors, could still take wickets in school matches. We have seen how in several Varsity matches of the past the game has been turned by a judicious spell of lob bowling, and the nervous tension in school matches can be even greater. Perhaps some schoolboys have from time to time contemplated the lob, but never had the nerve to try it out in a match. I can well remember how when I was working at Canford School, J.T. Hankinson and myself used to try out in the nets a form of under-arm bowling delivered like a back-handed lawn tennis stroke. That wonderful boy batsman, Iain P. Campbell was an eager participator in these lob experiments. Only once have I seen any reference to such a back-handed 'flip' delivery - in a letter to *The Cricketer* from D. Kirkland. The resulting spin was prodigious.

Well known at Canford at about this time was R.N. Exton, a first-class cricketer, whose off-spin bowling was ended by an attack of polio. His comments on having to relearn to bowl with the other hand are most interesting. He had originally heard about lob bowling from a Clifton master R.P. Keigwin who had batted against Simpson-Hayward. Exton set about a new cricket career with his left-handed lobs which he bowled consistently from 1950 to 1975. He writes: "I had two stock deliveries - an underhand Chinaman bowled with a follow-through rather than a flip, and a leg-spinner bowled from between fingers one and two, exactly as I had bowled my old off-break. 'Flight' was hard to achieve. The Chinaman was difficult to score off, because it kept low. The leg-spinner seldom came off the wicket at sufficient pace and was therefore vulnerable to the off-side slash to which field placing was a problem in view of the need to put several men on the leg." He also added: "It is a mistake to assume that under-arm bowling is slow bowling. The delivery of the fast ball in Bowls which is aimed at the jack illustrates the way in which speed can easily be achieved with a full swing."

May I be forgiven for ending on a brief personal note: in the first match in which I ever played, between two 5-a-side teams of seven-year olds, neither side scored a run off the bat, but as our opponents bowled several wides, and we bowled none, we had a handsome victory. As captain (like William Clarke) I bowled throughout the innings (which lasted under 10 minutes) and clean bowled all the other side. I can see myself now standing at the start of my run, right arm outstretched as though taking aim with the left eye closed, then fast in with those deadly straight grubs.

My method seems somewhat to have resembled that of Mr Luffey 'the highest ornament of Dingley Dell'. *The Pickwick Papers* tell us how he retired a few paces behind the wicket and applied the ball to his right eye for a few seconds: "Play! suddenly cried the bowler, the ball flew from his hand straight and swift towards the centre stump of the wicket.' Mr Dumkins, however, "on the alert", was able to divert Mr Luffey's first ball over the heads of the crouching 'scouts'. My bowling on this occasion proved more successful than that of Mr Luffey.

Later at my prep school Hydneye House, St Leonards on Sea, I continued to bowl under-arm for the under-Eleven colts team. Next year I changed without any trouble to over-arm and took wickets for the 1st XI. I am sure that practice with those lobs helped to create control and accuracy. My Headmaster, Mr E.G. Maltby, was a keen cricketer and we certainly had a lob bowler in the XI in my time. He was Bobby de Quincey who later won a golf Blue at Oxford.

I suggest no comparisons, but Spofforth bowled under-arm up to the age of 11, when he saw Tarrant's fast bowling in 1863-4, and decided to copy him. There has been one recent lob incident well worth the telling. The Australian Under-19 team were playing the N.A.Y.C. at Market Harborough in August 1991. The game was 'dead' when the incoming Australian batsman Greg Hayne made a jocular bet that he would score 50 off 20 balls. He was making good progress, and Jason Harrison, an off-spinner, was bowling; he bowled the sixth ball of one over so loosely that it was called wide by the umpire, but Hayne chased the ball into the outfield at fine-leg, and struck it to the boundary, whereupon the umpire cancelled the wide and awarded four runs for the hit.

The English captain, Justin Inglis, went over and facetiously remarked to the bowler that if he was going to bowl as badly as that he might as well try bowling under-arm. The bowler took him at his word, informed the umpire and the batsman that he was going to bowl under-arm, and so delivered what was really an illegal seventh ball of the over; the umpire had clearly forgotten the cancelled sixth ball wide. The batsman hit out full-bloodedly at this lob ball, missed it, and was given out lbw.

Inglis and Harrison were both reprimanded for their actions, but the lob ball had not been bowled in any unseemly form of protest; it was more of a joke, though Hayne had possibly sullied the atmosphere by his boastful announcement of his intended quick fifty. His action, the captain's remark, the under-arm ball, and the umpiring error all go to make up a wonderful example of the vagaries of the game.

Just when it seemed that in all levels of cricket any future under-arm bowling night be confined to the occasional unseemly 'protest' lob, an article by Scyld Berry in *The Daily Telegraph* (9th June, 1994) was entitled "Lobsters could still have a part to play." This enterprising article happily enabled me to make contact with a cricket club called 'The Lobsters'. Founded as long ago as 1952 it consists mostly of masters, parents and friends connected with Clifton College Preparatory School. The constitution insists that in every match at least one over in any innings must be bowled by a Lobster, delivering the ball "in the original under-arm manner perfected by early cricketing exponents". These lobs almost always produce wickets.

I quote from 'The Chief Lobster', Tony Milligan: "The most effective Lobsters have been left-handed, bowling over the wicket. The usual technique involves pitching the ball . . . in such a way that the batsman has to cope with the unfamiliar flight, pace and bounce. Spin is usually achieved by bowling with a straight arm and a sudden wrist and finger movement, anti-clockwise for leg-spin and clockwise for off. This does allow for backspin too. Obviously a variation of flight can disrupt the batsman's rhythm, and often impatience gets the better of him. We have used the huge arching full lob that the batsman has to smash in tennis style, but somehow that denies the values of other subtleties. I particularly enjoy the rare stumpings or even the lbw as the more humiliating fates of new victims. But the most dramatic and pleasing for spectators is the running catch on the boundary, a more common occurrence."

The spirit of Lobsters cricket has traditionally been one of good fellowship, involvement for all whatever their cricketing abilities, and success without sacrificing these essentials. This spirit and its unusual bowling feature has made the club extremely popular both to spectators and to the opponents met with at home and on an annual cricket tour.

73

Chapter 7

Some Hopes and Opinions

Though this story of under-arm bowling over the last seventy years has been one of steady and sad decline, a number of distinguished cricketers and writers have advocated its revival. This may be crying in the wilderness, and has not met with much success, but it shows a considered opinion.

"It is really extraordinary how helpful to his side even a bad lob bowler may sometimes be . . . it seems to me a great pity that lob bowling is not more cultivated." Lord Harris - *A Few Short Runs* (1921).

"It should not be forgotten that a lob bowler can be very useful on sun-baked wickets." Warwick Armstrong - *The Art of Cricket* (1922).

"If one or two of our good University bats who don't pretend to bowl took the time and the patience to practice for an hour or two a day assiduously in a net, they would soon have much better fun. For they would join in the bowling, and might win a Varsity match for their side." S.M.J. Woods - *Reminiscences* (1925).

"The death of Walter Humphreys (in 1924) emphasises a striking change that has come over modern cricket. Humphreys could not be described as the last of the lob bowlers - Mr Jephson and Mr Simpson-Hayward flourished after his day was done - be he was the last who filled the public eye. . . I am not inclined to think that lobs, however good, would be very effective against present-day batsmen, but their entire disappearance from first-class cricket is a loss. A decently-good lob bowler might still from sheer novelty and force of contrast turn the fortune of any public-school game, or even, perhaps, the University match. Apparently no one thinks it worthwhile to give the subject serious attention, but an Eton or Harrow boy who bowled lobs really well would, I fancy, reap his reward at Lord's." Sydney Pardon, Editor, *Wisden*, 1925.

"Two county captains of my acquaintance say they would willingly make use of lob bowling in an emergency, e.g. when two stodgy batsmen have dug themselves in, but they have nobody in their sides with any practical knowledge of it. If an expert were available, one of them admitted, the attitude of the crowd would have to be considered. . .The writer has studied this lost art ever since he was at his 'prep', and in the course of an obscure career has taken over 1500 wickets. He has never bowled in a county match, but has beguiled a number of county batsmen into getting themselves out. . . It is the psychological factor - unusualness - which would make under-arm bowling dangerous in these days." Extract from an unsigned article - *The Times* 1937.

"There is still another type of ball which although never practised in these modern days would, I am convinced, be very destructive, if perfected: the lob or under-arm. I have often wondered why it is so abandoned and neglected. It has been successful in the highest class of cricket, and would be so again, if anyone bowled it really well. . . Before retiring from cricket I have half a mind to develop the lob myself." C.F. Root, *A Cricket Pro's Lot* 1937.

"A first-class lob bowler would undoubtedly take plenty of wickets today, even in first-class cricket." Christopher Sly, *How to Bowl Them Out*, 1948.

"There is no reason to suppose that a good under-arm spin bowler would not be very efficient now. It is a great pity that under-arm bowling in first-class cricket should have become virtually extinct since the 1914-1918 War. With the aid of the great spin that is possible underhand, plus the unusual flight, it would seem likely that a really good under-arm bowler of the Simpson-Hayward calibre might well prove extremely successful today. The game is undoubtedly the poorer for the extinction of this kind of 'trundler', and it is to be hoped that this loss is temporary rather than permanent." Trevor Bailey and Denys Wilcox, *Cricketers in the Making*, 1950.

"If any budding cricketer should chance to read (about Jephson's and Simpson-Hayward's success in the Gentlemen *v* Players matches) he may be tempted to copy these two bowlers. I am certain that he would, if he could attain their skill, be a very useful adjunct to any side." P.F. Warner, *Gentlemen v Players*, 1950.

"Why do we not educate one of our main Test match batsmen, Mr Peter May or even Mr Hutton, to bowl decent lobs: I guarantee it would pay. I played against

Punter Humphreys, though not against William Clarke, and I found Punter decidedly unpleasant: such a contrast in flight and spin to George Lohmann or William Attewell. Please, I know what I am talking about. C.B. Fry, *The Cricketer*, 1954.

"Today the best opening for a lob bowler would be in University cricket: a young and athletic fielding side is required as support and a captain shrewd in his field placing." Scyld Berry, *The Cricketer*, 1973.

In reply to enquiry by a Mr Barr about lob bowling (he had read about Molony), Alf Gover wrote: "Mr Barr would be putting the clock back if he could really master the art of lob bowling, but I see no reason why this type of bowling should not get wickets in Club cricket." He goes on to explain in full detail how to learn this art, and how to master each type of under-arm delivery. He had given it much thought. Alf Gover, *The Cricketer*, 1979.

Index

This is an index of the names of those 130 cricketers who are known to have delivered balls bowled under-arm in a first-class match.

Hornby, A. N.

Humphreys, W. A.

Humphreys, W. A. Jun.

Iddison, R.

Illingworth, R.

Iverson, J. B.

Jephson, D. L. A.

Lambert, W.

Leatham, H. W.

Liddicut, A. E.

Lockyer, T.

Lyon, B. H.

Lyttelton, Hon. A.

MacLaren, A. C.

McCanlis, W. ('Willis')

Marlar, R. G.

May, P. H.

Meyer, R. J. O.

Mobarak Ali

Molony, T. J.

Money, W. B.

Monkland, F. G.

Mordaunt, G. J.

Mortlock, W.

Osbaldeston, G.

Palairet, L. C. H.

Parr, George

Patiala, Maharajah of

Phillips, H.

Pickering, F. P. U.

Pinder, G.

Piton, J. H.

Ponsonby, J. H.

Pooley, E.

Quinton, F. W. D.

Read, W. W.

Reynolds, F. R.

Ridley, A. W.

Rose, W. M.

Round, J.

Sainsbury, E.

Seymour, Jas.

Simpson, R. T.

Simpson-Hayward, G. H. T.

Smith. C. L. A.

Spooner, R. H.

Stephenson, H. H.

Stevenson, A. J.

Stevenson, H. J.

Stoddart, A.E.

Sugg, F. H.

Suttle, K. G.

Thornton, A. J.

Thornton, C. I.

Tinley, R. C.

Tinley, V.

Townsend, A. F. M.

Townsend F.

Turner, A. J.

Vengsarkar, D. B.

Verity, H.	Willsher, E.
Walker, A	Winter, G. E.
Walker, I. D.	Wisden, J.
Walker, R. D.	Wood, J. B.
Walker, Tom	Woods, S.M.J.
Walker, V. E.	Wooller, W. W.
Warsop, T.	Wrathall, W.
Wilkinson, C. T. A.	Wynyard, E. G.
Williams, P. F. C.	Yardley, W.

Here is a further list of under-arm bowlers concerned with lesser cricket.

Andrews, W. R. H.	Halfyard, D. J.
Ashfield, C. R. W.	Harrison, J
Barnes, S. F.	Hollies, W.
Bradby, M. C.	I'Anson, M.
Bullock, ?	Mackay, J. R. S.
Burton, R. H. L.	Merchant, A.
Chaplin, R. M.	Nash, J. G.
Chappell, T. M.	Peel, E. B.
Day, D. A. S.	Rose, T.
Exton, R. N.	Shaw, R. J.
Furber, S.	Simpson, G.F.
Goodrich, T. C.	Willes, J.
Griffen, G. M.	

Bibliography

H. S. Altham, A History of Cricket, Allen & Unwin, 1926.

J. Arlott, A Book of Cricketers, Lutterworth Press, 1979.

J.Arlott & S.Brogden, The First Test Match, Phoenix House, 1950.

W.W. Armstrong, The Art of Cricket, Methuen, 1922.

F. S. Ashley-Cooper, Edward Mills Grace, Chatto & Windus, 1916.

P. Bailey et al, Who's Who of Cricketers, Guild, 1984.

T. Bailey & D. Wilcox, Cricketers in the Making, Hutchinson, 1950.

S. Barnes, P. Edmonds, A Singular Man, Kingswood, 1986.

B. Bearshaw, From the Stretford End, Partridge, 1990.

W. A. Bettesworth, The Walkers of Southgate, Methuen, 1900.

W. A. Bettesworth, Chats on the Cricket Field, Merritt & Hatcher, 1910.

W. P. Bolland, Cricket Notes, Trelawney Saunders, 1851.

J.M. Brearley, The Art of Captaincy, Hodder & Stoughton, 1985.

G. Brodribb, Next Man in, Souvenir Press, 1995.

W. Caffyn, Seventy one not out, Blackwood, 1899.

A.W. Carr, Cricket With The Lid Off, Hutchinson, 1935.

J. D. Coldham, Lord Harris, Allen & Unwin, 1983.

'Country Vicar', Cricket Memories, Methuen, 1930.

R. Daft, Kings of Cricket, Arrowsmith, 1893.

G. Fowler, Fox on the Run, Viking, 1988.

D. Frith, "My Dear Victorious Stod", Lutterworth, 1977

D. Frith, The Fast Men, Van Nostrand, 1975.

D. Frith, The Slow Men, Allen & Unwin, 1984.

F. Gale, The Game of Cricket, Swan Sonnerschein, 1887.

F. Gale, Echoes from Old Cricket Fields, Nutt, 1896.

G. Giffen, With Bat and Ball, Ward, Lock, 1898.

A.E.R. Gilligan, Sussex Cricket, Chapman & Hall, 1933.

Lord Harris, A Few Short Runs, Murray, 1921.

A. Hignell, History of Glamorgan Cricket Club, Helm, 1988.

A. S. Gardiner, The Old Crocks, The Office, 1917.

D. L. A. Jephson in Cricket, Country Life, 1903.

G. L. Jessop, A Cricketer's Log, Hodder & Stoughton, 1922.

A. E. Knight, The Complete Cricketer, Methuen, 1906.

J. A. Lester, A Century of Philadelphia Cricket, Univ. of Pennsylvania, 1951.

W. J. Lewis, The Language of Cricket, Oxford University Press, 1934.

E. V. Lucas (ed), The Hambledon Men, Oxford University Press, 1907.

M. W. Luckin, The History of South African Cricket, Hortor, 1915.

M. Marshall, Gentlemen and Players, Grafton, 1987.

G. D. Martineau, They Made Cricket, Museum Press, 1956.

A. Meredith, The Demon and the Lobster (D.L.A. Jephson), Kingswood, 1987.

Mary Russell Mitford, Our Village, Whitaker, 1824-32.

C.H.B. Pridham, The Charm of Cricket, Jenkins, 1949.

A. W. Pullin ('Old Ebor') Old English Cricketers, Blackwood, 1900.

A. W. Pullin ('Old Ebor'), Alfred Shaw, Cricketer, Cassell, 1902.

J. Pycroft, The Cricket Field, Longmans, Green, 1859

J. Pycroft, Cricketana, Longmans, Green, 1865.

K. S. Ranjitsinhji, The Jubilee Book of Cricket, Blackwood, 1897.

R. S. Rait-Kerr, The Laws of Cricket, Longmans, Green, 1950.

C.F. Root, A Cricket Pro's Lot, Arnold, 1937.

I. Rosenwater, 100 Notable Cricket Quotations, Deutsch, 1995

E. H. D. Sewell, Overthrows, Stanley Paul, 1946.

S. Sly, How to Bowl Them Out, Thorsons, 1948.

A. G. Steel & R. H. Lyttelton, Cricket, Longmans, 1888.

R. Streeton, P.G.H. Fender, a Biography, Faber, 1981

H. Strudwick, 25 Years Behind the Stumps, Hutchinson, 1926.

P. Trevor, Problems of Cricket, Sampson, Low, 1907.

P. F. Warner, The Book of Cricket, Dent, 1911.

S. M. J. Woods, My Reminiscences, Chapman & Hall, 1925.

also:-   *Scores & Biographies*
       Wisden Cricketers' Almanack
       Wisden Cricket Monthly
       The Cricketer
       Cricket. A Weekly Record of the Game

In the Books mentioned above by Bettesworth, Gardiner, Meredith, Lord Harris, Trevor and Woods there are whole chapters concerned with under-arm or lob bowling. To show the extent in which even in recent times there has been an interest in under-arm bowling here is a list of articles on the subject;

Lobs - editorial in *The Cricket Field*, July 9, 1892

Lobs - E.B. Osborn in *The Times*, August 21, 1909

Lobsters - Cecil Headlam in *The Cricketer Annual 1922/23*, p21

Under-arm; First & Last - Richard Binns in *The Cricketer Annual 1936/37*, p73

Under-hand Bowling - A Lost Art - anon, *The Times*, August 28, 1937

Guile, or the Under-arm Method - Oliver Warner in *The Cricketer*, July 18, 1942

Plea For the Lob Bowler - C.H.B.Pridham in *The Cricketer Spring Annual 1948*

The Last Professional Lobster - J.D.Coldham in *The Cricketer*, May 15, 1954, p164

William Clarke and the Case for Under-hand - G.D.Martineau in *The Cricketer*, May 26, 1956, p180

Lobs - Past and Future? - Scyld Berry in *The Cricketer*, November 1973, p71

Back to the Lob Bowler - A.R. Gover in *The Cricketer*, April 1979, p77

The Lobster - D.L.A. Jephson - A. Bradbury in *The Cricketer*, April 1981, p57

The Lobster - Cricket Dido - P.Wynne-Thomas in *The Cricketer*, May 1983, p37

Lobsters Could Still Have a Part to Play - Scyld Berry in *The Daily Telegraph*, June 9, 1994